MODERN JEWELER'S

CONSUMER GUIDE TO COLORED GEMSTONES

Copyright© 1990 by Modern Jeweler Magazine,
a division of Vance Publishing Corporation

Library of Congress Catalog Card Number 89-22478
ISBN 0-442-00153-3

Printed in the United States of America

Distributed to the book trade by Van Nostrand Reinhold

Van Nostrand Reinhold
115 Fifth Avenue
New York, New York 10003

Van Nostrand Reinhold International Company Limited
11 New Fetter Lane
London EC4P 4EE, England

Van Nostrand Reinhold
480 La Trobe Street
Melbourne, Victoria 3000, Australia

Nelson Canada
1120 Birchmount Road
Scarborough, Ontario M1K 5G4, Canada

16 15 14 13 12 11 10 9 8 7 6 5 4 3 2 1

Library of Congress Cataloging-in-Publication Data

Federman, David.
   Modern jeweler's consumer guide to colored gemstones / David
Federman; with photographs by Tino Hammid.
      p. cm.
   ISBN 0-442-00153-3
   1. Precious stones—Handbooks, manuals, etc.   I. Title.
TS752.F387 1989
553.8—dc20   89-22478
                                                  CIP

The author and publisher have exercised their best judgement in selecting data to be
presented in this book, have reported in good faith the information from the sources, and
have made every reasonable effort to make the data presented accurate and authoritative. But
neither the author nor the publisher warrants the accuracy or completeness of the information
contained in this book or assumes liability for its fitness for any particular purpose or use.
Readers have the responsibility to seek expert advice for their specific applications.

CONSUMER GUIDE TO
COLORED GEMSTONES

DAVID FEDERMAN

PHOTOGRAPHS BY TINO HAMMID

VNR VAN NOSTRAND REINHOLD
_____ New York

Gemstones

... have intrigued us since the beginning of time.

Desired for their rarity and natural beauty, gemstones have been valued as objects of personal adornment and symbols of wealth and status by every culture throughout history.

Occurring in a remarkable variety of colors, from subtle pastels to brilliant hues, gemstones make a personal statement that captures and expresses your individuality with sparkle and style. Worn as accessories, collected, or given as gifts, the beauty and enduring value of natural colored gemstones make them desirable treasures to enjoy today and pass on to future generations.

The following collection of articles and photographs is a treasury of fascinating gemstone information. As sponsor of this publication, the American Gem Trade Association suggests that you supplement your knowledge and enhance your appreciation of gemstones by visiting retail jewelers who can help you ...

"Add More Color to Your Life
... With Natural Colored Gemstones."

TABLE OF CONTENTS

INTRODUCTION

Since early 1989, a gem dealer I've known for years has been calling me every few weeks to brief me on mounting mayhem in Colombia's lucrative emerald market. The troubling gist of these calls is always this: There is a full-fledged turf war going on between that South American country's bustling drug and gem trades for control of its emerald export business. According to this dealer and several others, anywhere from two to four thousand emerald industry people, mostly miners and dealers, have been murdered since 1980. No doubt the gem sector, itself never gun shy, has retaliated in full and in kind. After all, the two groups have banded together in an intermittent alliance against a common enemy—Communist guerillas—with results the CIA would envy.

I mention this bloodshed because of something the gem dealer once said to me: "I bet you never think of what a gem has to go through to get to a jewelry store."

He's right.

I tend to think of colored stones as things of beauty, not objects of gruesome power struggles between mining kingpins and drug lords. Can you blame me, or anyone with insider knowledge, if a gem sheds any connection with its past once sculpted by a cutter into the glittering marvel we see in a jeweler's showcase? Like Odysseus listening to the sirens' song, we become victims of an aesthetics-induced amnesia. All we can—or care to—remember is the gem's particular dazzle. Just by dint of the fashioning feat called cutting, a tiny rock is transformed into the world's most concentrated and prized form of wealth—as well as its most enduring and universal status symbol.

Gems have always had such stature. For thousands of years, these morsels of magnificence have inspired exploration and conquest. The Sumerians of ancient Mesopotamia traversed Asia to find lapis lazuli. Nero sent an army to northern Europe in search of amber. The Spaniards dispatched conquistadors to South America for emeralds. And a little more than a century ago, the British annexed part of Burma to take control of its famed ruby tracts.

Pardon me if the preceding sounds like over-romanticized gem investment propaganda. It's just hard to deny a resonance of near-worshipful admiration for gems that spans the entirety of human history and links the present to the past and, I'm quite sure, the future. True, few nations today keep gems as part of their national treasuries. And the thought of finding this mineralogical booty (in any other than diamondiferous form) is far from uppermost in the plans of most of the world's major mining companies.

INTRODUCTION

But today there is a subtle yet undeniable undercurrent of investment jewelry buying around the world. Smart money, in Asia and Europe especially, seems strongly aware of gems as portable stores of wealth. There is no other way to explain the rapid emergence of high-fashion custom jewelry markets for once-ignored gems like pink sapphire and indicolite (pure-blue tourmaline). Affluent consumers are taking to colored stones that combine the two classic gem attributes of beauty and rarity but that don't (not yet anyway) cost an arm and a leg. And a growing number of jewelers are stocking these exotic species.

The end result: The "rainbow revolution," a term coined in the 1970s when this demand for a wider range of colored gemstones began.

But now that the revolution in colored stone demand is here, there is an equally revolutionary demand for product information, possibly a spillover from other areas of retailing such as home electronics. Consumers are increasingly hesitant to spend money on gemstone jewelry unless such purchases are justified in terms of quality and value.

Years ago, merchants rarely said much about the gems they sold except to arouse interest by repeating shop-worn bits of folklore about them. That kind of information is hardly adequate in an age when many gem species are either heated, irradiated, oiled, dyed and plasticised to improve color, appearance and/or durability—occasionally all three. Some of these enhancements are permanent, others are not. Consumers need to know which if any of these touch-up methods have been applied to gems they are buying and what precautions they must take as a result when wearing or cleaning them.

But that's only the beginning of the shopper's product information needs. Whether or not a gem has been beautified, consumers want to know the pros and cons of ownership before buying. Are stones durable? What special care and handling do they require?

To help jewelers meet their customers' need for basic gemstone product information, *Modern Jeweler*, a jewelry trade magazine that debuted in 1901, launched a monthly column called Gem Profile in April 1983. The idea behind the column was to give on-the-run jewelers a short, lively essay and a suitable-for-framing photograph highlighting each and every gem of consequence to consumers, collectors and connoisseurs—the three main jewelry store patron groups. These essays, in turn, were to be used to train employees and also educate customers.

To accomplish these goals, each Gem Profile was designed to serve as a mini-course in gem appreciation—a radical departure in terms of matter and manner from jewelry trade and gemology journal gem writ-

INTRODUCTION

ing of the past. Not only did this new kind of essay call for brevity, clarity and simplicity, it called for a new approach to colored stones—one that viewed them as commodities rather than minerals.

From the outset, we veered sharply away from the dry, technical style of the well-versed gemologist and opted for the leaner, more literate one of the seasoned reporter. Then, to make sure readers had a clear idea of each gem's aesthetic pinnacle, we commissioned the well-known gem photographer Tino Hammid to supply a photograph for each profile. His superb images helped to make Gem Profile the most successful regular feature in *Modern Jeweler*'s history and to earn it two Jesse H. Neal awards, the highest honor in business press journalism.

In 1988, the fifth year of Gem Profile, demand for a permanent reference collection of these essays led Vance Publishing Corp., *Modern Jeweler*'s parent company, to publish the first five years' essays in a hardcover collection called "The First 60." Jewelers then asked us for an affordable paperback reprint that they could offer to customers. We decided on more than a mere reprint. We decided to revise and update each profile to make it as relevant to shoppers as possible. Hence the new title: "*Modern Jeweler*'s Consumer Guide to Colored Gemstones."

A little on the book "The First 60" has become. Our guiding principle in rewriting it was as old as the profile approach is new: Do to others as you would have them do to you. In other words, we decided to tell the reader, usually a jewelry industry outsider, exactly what any trade insider would expect to be told. So you'll read, where important, about the drug wars or other geopolitical dramas which affect the supply of the gem being discussed. You'll also learn of any enhancements, both legitimate and illegitimate, commonly performed on the gem under scrutiny. And, of course, we haven't skimped on vital history.

Last, but far from least, we've addressed the well-being of gems by discussing potential problems such as cracking or fading that a few delicate gem species are subject to if worn or handled improperly. Please keep in mind, however, that what we say about care and handling is meant to alert readers to possible hazards, not offer a guaranteed prescription for trouble-free ownership. No matter what kind of gem you buy, consult with your jeweler about the preservation of its beauty. It's a beauty that nothing else gives, the product of a collaboration between man and nature that is as old as man—or, at least, as old as his unique ability to craft objects whose main purpose is to inspire awe.

David Federman, July 1989

BRAZILIAN ALEXANDRITE

An acquaintance of mine, a Los Angeles-based specialist in Brazilian gems, still can't forget the moment in May 1987 when he confirmed the rumors he'd been hearing for months about a spectacular find of alexandrite in Minais Gerais, Brazil's province of gem plenty. "A dealer showed me a 400-piece parcel weighing 126 carats of which 35 stones were between 1 and 2½ carats," he recounts. "That was way more than all the alexandrite I had seen in the previous five years."

But the parcel wasn't just good news from a quantity standpoint. Its quality was equally impressive.

"The best of the stones were as good as, if not better than, any pieces I had ever seen," he continues. "I understood at a glance why Brazil's new alexandrite deposit is the most talked-about colored stone find of the decade."

Other dealers swaddle their first impressions of this new-lode color-change chrysoberyl in similar enthusiasm. It's hard not to once you see some—and realize that what is easily the world's most glorified connoisseur gem now has its first chance to score big with commoners, too.

NEW PRESTIGE FOR BRAZIL

Alexandrite is a fairly modern gem, unknown before 1830, when it was found in Russia's Ural Mountains. Since its two color states, green and red, were the same as the host country's military colors, and since its year of discovery was that in which Czar Alexander II came of ruling age, jewelry tradesmen named the chrysoberyl "alexandrite" as a tribute. That was a wise move for, in time, it became a very prized gem among Russia's aristocracy.

Alas, practically all of Russia's alexandrite was mined during the 19th century. But just when the species seemed headed for extinction, far larger deposits were found in Ceylon (now Sri Lanka), the island nation to the south of India. Later on, Brazil became still another contributor to world supply—although its stones didn't command respect until the recent discovery there.

Early in the 20th century, alexandrite aesthetics were far more a matter of debate than they are today, with dealers tending to be evenly divided in partisanship between Russian and Ceylonese stones. For example, gemology pioneer Max Bauer was unabashedly partial to the Ceylonese variety. In the last 50 years, however, the debate has become almost completely one-sided in favor of Russian material. Only once has this writer met an alexandrite expert who preferred Ceylonese to Russian stones.

BRAZILIAN ALEXANDRITE

Very likely, the trade's favoritism has a lot to do with the extreme rarity of Russian material, a key component of its value, although dealers have sworn to us that their preference was based purely on beauty. In any case, Russia is now to alexandrite what Burma is to ruby. No wonder, then, that we occasionally hear rumors, none confirmed, that the Soviets are actively prospecting for alexandrite.

Just in case they are, however, the news from Brazil may prompt them to put down their picks and shovels. Most dealers familiar with the new Brazilian alexandrite swear the best of it surpasses any Russian stones they have ever seen. If enough people eventually share this conviction, a distinct possibility, the gem shibboleth that holds Russian alexandrite the exemplar for this species will be shattered—and with it the rationale for the hefty prices fine Russian alexandrite commands. This is why we expect a purist backlash in the near future. A lot is at stake if new sentiments about Brazilian alexandrite take hold.

Already prices for new-find Brazilian alexandrite are scaling the heights. On a per-carat basis, dealers are charging as much for top-grade 1- to 2-carat stones as they were a short while back for alexandrites of 10 carats or more from Sri Lanka, the second-ranked source for this gem. Indeed, one dealer who sold what by Sri Lankan standards is an exceptional 20-plus-carat stone just before news broke of the Brazilian find, now considers himself lucky to have done so. "It was a fine stone but not in a league with what I've been buying recently from Brazil," he confides.

ANATOMY OF AN ADVANTAGE

As anyone who has seen the new alexandrite knows, these stones challenge common experience with this species. Although famous for changing color from green in sunlight to red in incandescent light, few alexandrites actually make a full-fledged color change. Usually there is bleed-through from one color state to another or too much color impurity to start with to permit any significant change. Because total color-change alexandrites are so very seldom seen, the trade thinks it axiomatic that in this species, such a characteristic is a rarity.

Now Brazil has raised trade expectations considerably because its new-find alexandrite excels at 100% color change. "The completeness of the color change in most of the material is one of the most amazing things about it," says a gem buyer with a major importer of the new alexandrite. "In Sri Lankan stones, there always seems to be an undertone of secondary brown or yellow."

BRAZILIAN ALEXANDRITE

Furthermore, the Brazilian stones boast admirable color richness. Greens in smaller sizes tend to be yellowish while those in larger stones are bluish. As for the red, the gem buyer compares it to the violet color of rhodolite in smaller stones and that of rubellite in larger pieces. One very lovely 2.53-carat stone shown to us by a dealer in California turned from a deep green to a luscious raspberry red.

THE JOYS AND SORROWS OF PLENTY

There are other virtues that endear Brazil's new-find alexandrite to dealers, including its better-than-usual clarity. But by far the most oft-cited plus after color change is availability. Nobody knows how much material has been cut. But insider estimates range from 5,000 to 10,000 carats, a staggering number for a gem as rare as alexandrite. What's more, a significant number of cut stones, some think as many as 30%, are 1 carat or more in size.

All this spells relative plenitude for a gem never thought of as plentiful. And that's got some dealers worried. "Half the charm of alexandrite to collectors is its rarity," says one New York fine gem specialist. "Since collectors are the backbone of the alexandrite market, will ready availability of fine specimens chase them away? And if so, what will that do to prices?"

Those are good questions, ones it is far too soon to answer. At present, the new-find alexandrite mining area, known as Nova Era City, is closed after some bloody claim site disputes, the kind said to typically accompany major gem strikes in Brazil.

Nevertheless, most dealers expect mining to re-commence and production to continue on the hearty side for at least a few more years. And while it is true that continued large production could rattle connoisseurs, dealers feel the opportunity to mainstream alexandrite, the June birthstone, would more than compensate for any loss of collector interest.

RUSSIAN ALEXANDRITE

Ever since stones from a splendid new Brazilian find started making their way to market in early 1987, much conventional wisdom about alexandrite has had to be chucked.

Take, for instance, the common trade assumption that South America is good for nothing but the most inferior variety of this color-change chrysoberyl. Rather than turning green in sunlight and red in incandescent light as model alexandrite is supposed to do, Brazil's stones are accused of almost always stopping far short of green at olive and far short of red at brown. "Don't mention Brazil and alexandrite to me in the same breath," sniffed one San Francisco antique and estate jewelry dealer who had not heard about the new find when we called to ask him about it.

Ironically, his description of the ideal alexandrite color change—rich blue green to strong purple red—fit what we have observed in the best of Brazil's new breed. Yet this expert maintained that such colors were found only in Russian stones from Siberia and the Ural Mountains mined almost exclusively in the 19th century. So did the owner of a major antiquities gallery on New York's Fifth Avenue who was also unaware of the find. His reaction to the news of Brazil's latest alexandrite: "We would welcome more stones with the Siberian colors."

That's what dealers swept off their feet by the new find are counting on: favorable comparison of their new alexandrites with the grandest stones produced by Russia. Why are Russian stones so admired in the first place?

THE TIFFANY CONNECTION

To those familiar with Russian stones besides alexandrite, Russia is synonymous with the ultimate in species excellence. It is common in the trade to hear amethyst described as possessing Siberian color. And dealers familiar with both the demantoid and tsavorite varieties of green garnet will tell you Russia's Ural Mountain demantoids are far superior to East Africa's tsavorites. So powerful is the mystique of Russian gems that one antiquities expert who used to work for a famous Boston-based estate goods house swears the finest emeralds he has ever seen came from Russia—this from a man who is intimately versed in emerald from every origin known.

But of all Russian gems, it is alexandrite that is the most coveted. The trouble is that mining of this gem in Russia lasted less than 100 years and probably peaked late in the 19th century. From the very beginning, Russian alexandrite led a charmed life. Discovered in 1830 on Czar Alex-

RUSSIAN ALEXANDRITE

ander II's birthday, the stone was named after him because its green and red colors were those of the motherland.

Although the gem quickly found favor in the jewelry salons of St. Petersburg and Paris, it was Tiffany that seems to have done the most to popularize it in the world at large (as it also did for demantoid). Gemologist George Kunz, the firm's audacious gem buyer, fell so in love with alexandrite that he travelled to Russia in search of it.

No one knows just how much of this then-rare gem Kunz bought in Russia, but it seems likely that as a result of his efforts Tiffany had reserves so considerable that it may have cornered the market for decades. Russian gems and jewelry expert Peter Schaffer of world-famous À La Vieille Russie, New York, says that more than 50% of the Russian alexandrite pieces that his firm has sold were made by Tiffany, nearly all of them center-stone rings, most dating from the 19th century, but some long after, one even as late as the 1950s. Interestingly, many of the other pieces with Russian alexandrite that Schaffer has sold were made in England during the Victorian era and feature groupings of small stones. "Tiffany preferred larger sizes," he says.

BIG ISN'T BEAUTIFUL

What Schaffer means by "larger" is not exactly what the word means when applied to, say, sapphire or amethyst. Although he has seen Russian alexandrites of 30 and 40 carats, Schaffer says they almost never impressed him. "In top alexandrite, the stone turns from deep green to deep red as if you were watching a traffic light change colors," he says. "Past around 8 carats, you rarely see Siberian stones that have the right colors or change them completely enough."

Those who desired alexandrite in truly large sizes with good color change have long relied on Sri Lanka. For some dealers, these stones are actually superior to the Russian variety. A New York lapidary says he prefers Sri Lankan to Russian alexandrite because its green veers toward yellow rather than blue and its red is more bronze than purple.

This cutter belongs to a decided minority, especially since Brazilian stones highly evocative of the Russian type have come into the marketplace. Indeed, the similarity between South American and Russian alexandrite is now so great some dealers fear attempts to pass off Brazil's best as bona fide Siberian. To prevent such frauds, dealers suggest that gemologists who specialize in country of origin work begin to publish studies which show dealers and jewelers how to differentiate between the two varieties via microscopic examination.

RUSSIAN ALEXANDRITE

While acknowledging the strong color resemblances between Brazilian and Russian alexandrites, specialists in late 19th century antique jewelry where Siberian stones are most often found nowadays say Russian stones have slightly deeper tones and more saturate colors. One Tiffany jewelry expert who has seen scores of Siberian alexandrites and is fond of the new Brazilian stones describes the latter as "more watery" in appearance. By this somewhat subtle distinction, he means they seem clearer, more transparent. But the point is this: No matter how refined the differences between Brazilian and Russian stones are, they can be told apart. So jewelers need not fear country of origin frauds if buying from reputable dealers.

With their greens and reds so reminiscent of Russian stones, it is hardly surprising to find prices for 2- to 3-carat Brazilian stones already reaching levels among dealers that are on a par with far larger and rarer stones from Sri Lanka. Will relatively abundant Brazilian alexandrites be able to justify prices nearing the same high plateau where important dealers in Russian stones already resist them for far rarer Siberian pieces?

Perhaps not in America. But one shouldn't forget that the primary buyers of alexandrite for some time now have been the Japanese—the world's most dogged devotees of phenomenon stones such as cat's-eye, black opal and, of course, alexandrite. Especially fond of sizes between 2 and 4 carats, the Japanese have so far swallowed the high prices being asked for fine alexandrite under 4 carats—whether of Siberian origin or simply Siberian color. As long as they remain hooked on alexandrite, and as long as the dollar stays weak against the yen, U.S. dealers will have no choice but to pay more if they want a piece of the comeback action in this coveted chrysoberyl.

AMBER

Money doesn't grow on trees, but gems do. Or did.

Some 25 to 40 million years ago, in what is now the Baltic region of Europe (Poland, Latvia and Lithuania especially), towering tropical pine forests began to sweat sap profusely. Globs of this sticky, aromatic resin poured down the sides of trees, often trapping leaves, twigs, bark and, occasionally, insects in their paths, and meanwhile snowballing in size. (The same process repeated itself during a later geological epoch in what is now the Dominican Republic and, still later, in what is now Tanzania.)

Imagine, for a moment, these forests with their bejeweled floors and tree trunks. What a spectacular sight they must have been. Eventually, continental drift and an ice age or two took these vast pine tracts underground where their resin globs hardened into a soft, warm, lustrous substance that looks and feels a lot like plastic.

More recently, within the last million years, Stone Age man discovered pieces of this fossilized sap washed up on the Baltic shores or floating farther out to sea. Inviting to the eye and sensuous to the touch, it was only a matter of time before mythopoeic early man imbued these sea jewels with supernatural properties (it was said they came from the sun) and used them for both wear and worship. This fascination continued into and past the dawn of civilization as the golden stone took on great value and significance to, among others, the Assyrians, Egyptians, Etruscans, Phoenicians and Greeks.

Love of amber is as old as mankind. Archaeologists have positively dated amber artifacts as far back as 5000 B.C. No other gem except, perhaps, the pearl, can rival amber for sustained ornamental usage and popularity. The gem has never really gone out of vogue. Between 1895 and 1900, one million kilograms of Baltic amber were produced for jewelry. And well into the 1920s, amber was second only to diamonds in terms of U.S. gem imports.

There are plenty of reasons why amber has enjoyed 70 centuries of adoration.

FROZEN TIME

To look at a piece of fine amber is to look at a miniature time capsule made and placed in the earth by nature herself. Incredibly, according to Patty C. Rice, author of "Amber: The Golden Gem of the Ages," more than 1,000 species of extinct insects and crustacea have been found in amber. Studying leaves, twigs and botanical debris found encased in this gem has helped to identify many forerunners of our modern conifers,

AMBER

not to mention plants and flowers. Most importantly, it has helped paleontologists reconstruct life on earth in its primal phases.

But besides preserving the pre-human past, amber resonates with human history. No other gem is so intricately intertwined with the development of civilization and the procession of past societies. Baltic amber was a mainstay of trade and commerce in early Europe and the adjoining Mediterranean region at least as far back as 3200 B.C., by which time Egyptian dynasty and Stonehenge priests were already burying it in tombs, presumably to enable its owners to have good fortune in the afterlife.

Given such veneration, it comes as no surprise that the quest for amber motivated conquest for thousands of years. For instance, the Phoenicians, perhaps the best-known and most enterprising of ancient mariner peoples, opened new sea routes to northern Europe in an attempt to obtain amber direct from, or at least, closer to its source. (By then amber was known as "gold of the north.") The Romans went one step further and sent armies to annex amber trading and producing areas. Indeed, wrote the great natural historian Pliny during the time of Nero (amber's most ardent addict), "The price of a figurine in amber, however small, exceeded that of a living, healthy slave."

The passion for amber wasn't merely pagan. Clear, colorless amber was considered the most desirable material for rosary beads throughout the Middle Ages. In fact, the amber rosary bead business was so big that certain orders of knights gained virtual monopolistic control of the gem. By 1400 A.D., the possession and sale of raw, unfashioned amber was illegal in much of Europe.

"BRAND X" SAPS

The Baltic region is to amber what Burma is to ruby: its most prized source. Ironically, amber connoisseurs talk almost as admiringly of a reddish-brown Burma amber, the hardest (3 on the Mohs scale) and thus the oldest of all amber yet discovered (the longer amber is buried, the harder it gets). Obviously, hardness, usually 1.5 to 2.5 on the Mohs scale, is not one of amber's strong points. But it more than compensates for its softness with a range of colors, numbering around 250, including very rare blue and green specimens from Sicily.

Aficionados divide amber into two main groups: clear and cloudy. The clear variety takes a high polish and is very much in demand, particularly in bead form in America. The cloudy type, most often likened to whipped honey in appearance, is preferred in Europe and North Africa.

AMBER

(Amber is popular among the Arabs.)

Believe it or not, Baltic origin is a selling point for amber. Stones from this region contain succinic acid and are known as succinites while those without are known as retinites. To the unaided eye, it is impossible to tell succinite from retinite amber.

It is equally difficult to tell amber from its natural, much more recently created substitutes, the most common of which is copal, formed in African forests within the last 1,000 years. Copal not only resembles amber in appearance, it also contains leaves and insects. To differentiate copal, put a drop or two of ether on the stone in question. If it's copal, it will turn sticky.

Nevertheless, don't let ether decide whether the stone is amber. If the stone stays hard, it could just as well be a fake as amber. Plastic look-alike amber has long been a problem, especially since the late 19th century and the advent of synthesized plastic imitations such as celluloid, bakelite, and, more recently, bernit, polystrene and polybern. Thankfully, hot-point testing can help in detection of these fakes. Trickier to detect is pressed, or reconstructed, amber that consists of fused natural amber pieces—often with insects inserted. Even all-natural amber is commonly oiled to remove cloudiness, as well as to darken and harden it. It is only fitting that the longest-coveted gem should be paid the supreme flattery of rampant adulteration and imitation.

AFRICAN AMETHYST

Although Africa has been producing amethyst for more than a decade, the news was pretty much of a trade secret until only a few years ago. Now, with this deep purple gem very much in vogue (it is also the February birthstone) jewelry manufacturers and retailers are specifying the African variety when ordering amethyst.

Not that they always get it.

To the contrary, stones labeled "African" stand more than a 50/50 chance of originating in Brazil (a beehive of amethyst mining) or Uruguay (a major new source). And despite an easy-to-perform test to distinguish natural from synthetic amethyst recently made public by the Gemological Institute of America, Santa Monica, Calif., parcels can still be salted with splendid replicas of nature manufactured in Russian and Japanese labs.

In short, Africa has become more a synonym than a source for amethyst of the best color and appearance being found. To be sure, the ideal for this quartz remains the Siberian variety. But since Siberia is consid ered a defunct source, stones from Africa now represent the point closest to the ideal that dealers can hope for.

Even specialists in South American amethyst concede that Africa currently sets the standard of excellence for this gem. "African stones are normally better than South American," says a Los Angeles cutter. "They've usually got a royal purple with reddish overtones that is very beautiful." This cutter admits he would like to sell African amethyst but says supplies of rough are too hard to come by and much too expensive when they are available.

Yet other amethyst dealers are willing to pay extra to get African material. "Money really isn't the problem," says a Seattle importer. "It's the waiting."

So it would seem. In July 1985, during a buying trip to Africa, a dealer promised him 100 kilos of Zambian amethyst rough. He received the first fifth of his order—20 kilos—18 months later.

What is it about African amethyst that makes dealers put up with so much to get it?

A PREFERENCE FOR DARK

African amethyst, like African aquamarine, tends to come in much smaller sizes than its South American counterparts. But what it lacks in size, it more than makes up for in color.

For some unknown reason, it is Africa's forte to cram incredible color intensity into small crystals. Until African amethyst and aqua came

AFRICAN AMETHYST

on stream in full force in the early 1980s, the market had to make do with, at best, medium color intensities for these gems in sizes under 3 carats. In fact, pale lilac shades, known in some quarters as "Rose of France," were often all that consumers got to see. Few knew the deep purple stones that inspired the Greeks to name the gem *amethystos*, which means "not intoxicated," and made them earnestly believe that drinking wine from amethyst cups would prevent drunkenness.

All that changed as demand for calibrated stones, generally under 2 carats, grew, and Africa's darker-toned amethyst and aqua gave manufacturers small stones that had deep, punchy colors—enough to allow the market to shift its preference in small sizes from medium to dark stones. If anything, African stones were often too dark, plagued by what gemologists at the American Gem Market System, Moraga, Calif., have dubbed "extinction," areas blacked out due to over-saturation of color.

Alas, small—both in terms of sizes and supplies—is just about all there is when it comes to African amethyst. Stones of 10 carats or more are rarities. And finding fine stones of 5 or 6 carats requires patience. Come to think of it, routine requests for decent-quality calibrated sizes may call for a search party.

And no wonder. An American dealer living in Zambia, Africa's principal producer of amethyst, who is one of two cutters in that country registered to buy rough from Mindico, the state-run gem sales agency, reports having been allocated a meager 5 kilos of amethyst for one entire year! Of this, only 5% was cuttable.

POOR PICKINGS FOR U.S.

This American might have received more goods if he were a big spender to begin with. Since he isn't, far more preferential treatment is being accorded to consortiums from countries including Taiwan, Japan and Germany willing to buy in tremendous bulk. As a result, smaller-fry rough buyers are squeezed out of the African market and must rely on secondary sources in places such as Hong Kong, Thailand and, recently, South Korea—the last coming on very strong as a cutting center for amethyst and irradiated blue topaz.

The goods made available to them from these sources are very often the rejects the consortiums put on the market after sorting through goods and taking the best for themselves.

Luckily for small dealers, a smattering of Zambian goods can somehow be found, as well as increasing but still minuscule production from Tanzania, Africa's next great hope for amethyst. Recently, Namibia has

AFRICAN AMETHYST

pitched in with excellent stones, but production is still limited and future supply a question mark.

Endless procurement difficulties help to explain why so many dealers give up the quest for bona fide African material and opt for ersatz African amethyst. Usually, this means South American goods shipped to the Far East where they are sold, presumably at a premium, as "Zambian."

Given the scarcity of true African amethyst, prices for it in commercial grades are generally 30% to 40% higher than those of its far more plentiful South American counterparts. At present, decent-quality calibrated African goods between ½ and 3 carats are all the rage. Manufacturers are using mostly oval, pear and, recently, heart shapes. But more offbeat fancy shapes such as the trillion and segment cut are coming on strong. This is understandable since amethyst is a strong fashion gem and such cuts are a growing trend.

However, it is highly unlikely that consumers will see African amethyst used for the increasingly voguish geometric shapes known in the trade as "fantasy" cuts. First developed in Germany, these shapes are now cut all over the world, including Korea, Brazil and America. Since artisanry, more than color, is these stones' primary attribute, those who make them have been willing to settle for medium-toned material from South America.

ANDALUSITE

Some gems seen to be victims of that oft-repeated childhood proverb: If you can't say anything nice, don't say anything at all. Andalusite, found principally in Brazil but named after Andalusia in Spain, its earliest source, is one of them.

For sure, this gem has its devotees. But most of them keep their devotion low-key and Platonic. With friends like that, it is hardly surprising that andalusite stays a victim of the silent treatment. Even those landmark studies of gemology, Max Bauer's "Precious Stones" and Robert Webster's "Gems," pay scant attention to this member of the silicate family.

Certainly, one can easily make a case against andalusite. For starters, stones are often afflicted by annoying amounts of gray and brown. Next, fine qualities are hard to find in sizes over 5 carats. No matter what the size, rutile needles are often visibly present, detracting further from this stone. Last, distinct cleavage (susceptibility to breaking along certain crystal planes) can pose a problem for neophyte setters.

Yet one can just as easily make a case *for* andalusite. At its best, it offers unique, lovely color—for very little money. "You don't look to andalusite to find perfection in any one color," says a Virginia collector and gem specialist. "You look to it to find vivid color contrast."

That's because andalusite is a pleochroic stone, meaning it gives off different colors when viewed in different directions. With most pleochroic stones, cutters try to minimize this effect, concentrating on obtaining one predominant color. For example, when cutting tanzanite, they will shoot for an optimal Kashmir blue, extinguishing as much as possible the stone's strong violet component.

Cutters change the rules when it comes to andalusite. Here they shoot to *maximize* pleochroism. The stone's two basic hues, yellowish green and orangy brown, aren't very often pleasing enough in themselves to emphasize one over the other. But when cut to be played off against each other, stones take on new life through sharp color contrast. The intensity of this contrast is what beauty in andalusite is all about. Yet this unique aesthetic makes andalusite an acquired taste.

THE "PHENOMENON" FALLACY

Education is the key to connoisseurship of andalusite. But it is hard to educate in print since its best colors are difficult to describe. Try to imagine, if you will, a cushion or emerald-cut stone with a pronounced middle area of a light, sometimes steely, yellow green that gives way abruptly on each side to sharply contrasting end areas of bronze or

ANDALUSITE

purplish orange-brown. This is how the dramatic color-play in this gem appeared in the finest specimens we were able to see.

While some dealers told us to look for pink in the brown, we observed it only in all-brown round stones and never in fancy shapes (where strong pleochroic effects are best emphasized)—at least not the ones shown to us. Occasionally, all-pink or all-green stones are cut, but the few we saw were rounds with very hazy, cloudy colors, of interest only to collectors.

However, we mention these pinkish-brown and grayish-green stones because it is their colors that most reminded us of those found in alexandrite, a color-change gem to which andalusite is so often compared that it is called "the poor man's alexandrite." If meant as a compliment, it is a backhanded one that virtually dooms andalusite's appeal, although it is clear that the gem may once have been sold as the far more costly chrysoberyl. Bauer hints as much in the 1909 edition of his book, "Precious Stones." Why the confusion?

Alexandrite is a chrysoberyl that changes color like a stoplight when viewed in different lighting conditions. In daylight, stones exhibit strong greens variously modified by yellow, brown and gray. At its best, this green can resemble that of a bluish-green tourmaline; at its worst, a light olive brown-green. Under artificial light, alexandrites display red, often modified by purple and brown. At its best, this red is raspberry-like; at its worst, a muddy purplish-brown. Because it changes body color in different lighting environments, alexandrite is classified as a "phenomenon" stone.

Andalusite, on the other hand, is not a "phenomenon" stone. It does not change color the way alexandrite does. It simply displays different colors at the same time, thanks, as we said, to its strong pleochroism and, of course, proper cutting. What's more, these colors bear some resemblance—but not a strong one—to those of alexandrite. For instance, the purplish orangy-brown of fine andalusite is a far cry from the raspberry red of fine alexandrite.

The same holds true in comparisons of commercial-grade stones. Due to improper orientation (cutting at a specific angle to a gem's optical axis), the pleochroic effect in commercial stones is weak or almost absent. Consequently, many parcels of fancy-cut andalusites exhibit a basic brownish yellow-green throughout with only flashes of orange at the ends. The main green color doesn't evoke the far more olive-green color of commercial alexandrite.

ANDALUSITE

A NARROW NICHE

As of now, andalusite jewelry is a rarity. The few jewelers who know about it tend to be colored stone specialists with training in gemology who stock it more out of curiosity than enthusiasm. As a result, their customers are far more likely to see it loose than mounted—and in a very small selection, possibly just one stone. That's hardly enough to inspire interest in the gem.

Yet, as our photograph of andalusite shows, the gem has a striking beauty that lends itself, we think, to jewelry usage. With a hardness of 7-7½ on the Mohs scale, andalusite also boasts durability. But bear in mind that sharp cleavages (stress areas within the gem's crystal structure) can make it a somewhat high-strung ring stone. Because andalusite is so seldom featured in jewelry, its cost will be quite reasonable—at least in sizes under 5 carats. And below 3 carats, where fine andalusite is the most abundant, it's downright inexpensive.

Therefore, low price, coupled with distinctive beauty, makes andalusite a perfect candidate for standout jewelry pieces. As one jewelry designer familiar with the gem put it: "The high color contrast makes it sure to get noticed. And isn't attracting attention what wearing jewelry is all about?"

Maybe. But the fact that so few suppliers carry andalusite has convinced many jewelers that it is too rare for anything but oddball usage. In reality, the gem is available in decent quantities in sizes up to 3 carats. Brazil remains a very steady producer of this gem, in small sizes especially, with backup supplies coming from Sri Lanka, long the leading secondary source. Between the two countries, there is enough fine andalusite for enterprising jewelers.

"I recently gave a gift of andalusite jewelry to a friend," relates a West Coast gem importer. "She says her stone received a lot of flattering attention, much more than she ever expected. This kind of reaction leads me to believe andalusite is a real sleeper."

AFRICAN AQUAMARINE

Recently, the decade-old battle between aquamarine and topaz—the prime movers among pastel-blue gems—has seemed so one-sided that some of America's fiercest aqua partisans are doubting, if still not deserting, the cause.

As the blue beryl has steadily lost ground in the United States to far less expensive but no less beautiful blue topaz, some firms that specialize exclusively in aqua have begun to pledge allegiance to both blues. And no wonder. Dealers who added the aqua stand-in to their inventories soon found that its sales amounted to 40% to 50% of those of aqua. One West Coast convert says the switch was not a matter of choice, but of facing the new reality of the American marketplace.

There, affordable is in, and the more affordable the better.

But the dealer didn't abandon aqua entirely. He didn't have to. Instead, he switched from expensive Brazilian material to new and far less expensive goods coming from Africa. Other aqua partisans did the same. It was just about the only way for U.S. dealers to stay in the aqua business.

Even before dealers moved en masse to topaz they had begun to snub the Brazilian variety, for years the American market's mainstay. The influx of new-breed aqua from African countries like Nigeria, Zambia and Zimbabwe that started in 1982 made it hard to resist. One New York gem dealer tells us almost all the aquas he buys now are African stones cut in Israel. "They have lovely deep colors never thought possible in 1- to 2-carat sizes and prices just as attractive," he declares.

Beautiful bargains in African aqua have hurt U.S. sales of South American stones, which rarely possess comparable richness of color in popular smaller sizes. And as sales of Brazilian aqua fall by the wayside, so have cherished notions about this gem as a whole.

SMALL, DARK AND HANDSOME

Truth is rarely absolute in the gem world. Gems from a newly discovered locality can challenge, even demolish, near-sacred notions about a species.

Until just recently, the gem world based its assumptions about aquamarine almost exclusively on acquaintance with the Brazilian variety. As a result, it was believed that aqua had to come in larger sizes, 10 carats or more, to realize its deepest, fullest color. True, deposits like the Santa Maria and Colonel Murta in Brazil yielded darker-color small stones, but such stones were the exception to the rule. On the whole, larger crystallization and bigger body mass were considered prerequisites for saturate-blue aquamarine.

AFRICAN AQUAMARINE

Then stones from Kenya, later followed by stones from Zimbabwe, Nigeria and Zambia, started appearing on the market. Most of them came from Germany, long a principal cutting center for African gems.

"African aqua broke all the rules," says a Seattle gem dealer. "We were seeing spectacular deep blue colors in stones as small as 50 points. Brazil had little or nothing to compete with these goods, as far as color goes, in sizes under 5 carats."

In no time at all, the Seattle dealer had switched from Brazilian to African goods in small sizes. One powerful inducement, besides deeper color, was lower cost.

"Aqua had been a popular inflation hedge in Brazil and prices were at all-time highs," he continues. "African material was available for far less money. This may have contributed to the collapse of the Brazilian aquamarine market in 1982."

The introduction of African aqua couldn't have come at a better time. Still in the throes of a recession, the U.S. jewelry market was shifting from larger free sizes to smaller calibrated ones. Using African aquas, jewelry makers could give consumers deeper colors in economical 1- to 2-carat sizes. Although the recession is over, this trend still holds sway today. However, signs point to a resurgence in somewhat larger sizes.

BACK FROM PLENITUDE

African aqua was not only a godsend for jewelry manufacturers. It gave a colored-stone cutting center like Israel a new lease on life just when supplies of Zambian emerald, for years practically the sole sustainer of Tel Aviv's precious colored stone market, began to dry up. For sure, Israel is not yet the force in aqua it is in emerald. But dealers who have seen Israeli-cut aquas describe the workmanship as superb.

The real power in African aqua is Idar-Oberstein, West Germany. A peer of Israel in terms of cutting, it has no peer in terms of supply. A tour of dealer storerooms there proves it. In one, we saw sack after sack overflowing with African aqua rough, enough, their owner said, to keep him going well into the next decade.

But you don't have to trek to Germany to find plenitudes of African aqua. Periodically, African miners have been known to dump rough on the U.S. market. Such an event happened in 1983-84 when the U.S. dollar was riding high. Hungry for cash, Nigerian miners sold rough at giveaway prices—often as little as one-fifth that of comparable Brazilian rough. Despite the far lower yields of Nigerian rough, dealers scooped up the material. Even Brazilians were taking advantage of the bonanza.

AFRICAN AQUAMARINE

BLUE AU NATUREL

Almost unnoticed in the early euphoria about African aqua was the fact that all, or almost all, of it has been spared heating, something obligatory for Brazilian material. Until the influx of African aqua, it had been a truism that virtually all aqua was treated.

Suddenly that truism was a half-truth. Many African aquas had already attained a desirable blue in the ground. So trips to the oven were unnecessary. True, some natural-blue stones had steel-gray overtones, but heating didn't help. Besides, the market began to adjust to African strains of blue. "Jewelers didn't like the dark green of Zambian emerald at first either," one dealer points out.

What took a little more getting used to were stones with heat-resistant tinges of green. According to gemologists, the green in African aqua is the result of chromium while that in Brazilian stones stems from iron. While heating can subdue the influence of iron, it doesn't alter chromium-induced colors.

Thus many of the aquas seen in Germany nowadays have a distinct green overtone. Although we find these stones attractive, purists still prefer all-blue stones. However, lower prices for greenish-blue aquas tempt some purists to experiment.

"It's ironic," one importer notes. "Africa may eventually force fresh acceptance of the natural color of most Brazilian aquas, a color dealers have been altering for decades."

BRAZILIAN AQUAMARINE

If aquamarine was spared the price pummelings of the 1981-85 jewelry industry recession, it is no thanks to America. There the gem's sales have been the weakest in decades—and are getting weaker. Mass volume jewelry manufacturers in the United States have jilted this blue beryl in favor of an overly abundant and less expensive look-alike: irradiated blue topaz. "It's a matter of economics," explains a Los Angeles gem cutter. Per-carat prices to jewelry manufacturers for bulk aqua are at least 10 times what they are for bulk blue topaz.

Elsewhere in the world, however, near-giveaway prices for blue topaz have not shaken jewelry-maker loyalty to aqua. If anything, they have strengthened allegiance to it. "In America, manufacturers want color, they want look," a dealer says. "But abroad they want lasting value."

By lasting value he means long-term appreciation. That's something irradiated blue topaz has always found it difficult to give. But now market surfeit and consequent cost-cutting threaten to make it the gem equivalent of the LCD watch, a technological marvel that once commanded hundreds of dollars and is readily available today for less than $5. In less than a decade, the price of blue topaz has dropped to around 10% of its original cost. That kind of relentless decline of value turns off jewelry buyers in big spender countries like Japan seeking strong asset value, as well as beauty, in the gems they purchase.

Aqua, on the other hand, is a proven performer in Asia and Europe. Even in America, prices for fine aqua during the worst of the early-to-mid-1980s recession held their own at levels only 20% below highs reached in 1980-81. That's more than can be said for fine ruby and sapphire.

What's more, aqua has rebounded from these modest declines on the international market. That's why dealers are selling so many fine aquas abroad. So should Americans develop a taste for fine aqua, they are in for a shock when they find out what it will cost to indulge this appetite.

THE PRICE POINT TRAP

America has never been a haven for fine aqua. Even in the brief heyday of gem investment back in 1980-81, few of the breed's best made their way into portfolios. Instead, medium-color larger stones were sold to investors who had no idea that aqua color could rival that of the deepest blue topaz. Such stones were almost always sold abroad at unflinching prices that easily topped those paid in America.

The situation remains the same today. Indeed, it has been aggravated by the U.S. dollar's chronic weakness against other currencies such as

BRAZILIAN AQUAMARINE

the yen and deutsche mark. Before the advent of irradiated blue topaz, America had to make do with low-end and commercial grades of aqua. Indeed, this country was a dumping ground for pale junk aqua, most of it from Brazil, the world's leading aqua producer, responsible, until the 1980s, for as much as 90% of annual caratage.

America's reputation as an aqua dump was primarily its own fault, the result of what one dealer calls "a rigid price point orientation." He means essentially this: U.S. jewelry makers don't buy according to quality, they buy according to price. Seen from that perspective, fine aqua has become an off-limits item to most American jewelry makers. Used to thinking of aqua as a semiprecious stone, they are shocked when they hear that 3- to 5-carat stones will cost them 100 times what look-alike irradiated blue topaz will. Such reactions have steered large numbers of superb aquas away from our shores. In their place, jewelers use deep-blue irradiated topaz.

Ironically, however, lack of experience here with fine aqua has discouraged consumption of that deepest of deep blue irradiated topaz, called "London Blue," that apes the most superb aqua color. Jewelers here unused to super-saturate aqua accuse this topaz of looking phony. Instead, they want medium sky-blue colors. But anyone who has seen collector specimens of Brazilian aqua from the famous but bygone Santa Maria deposit knows this gem can possess an extraordinarily deep electric blue that, dare we say it, invites comparison to dark irradiated blue topaz. From time to time throughout this decade, some comparably deep aqua has been mined in African countries such as Nigeria and Zambia. But very often deep blue African stones are grayish or steely blue, and, consequently, lack the warmth of Brazil's best.

Unfortunately, few Brazilian aquas boast color saturation in small sizes akin to even medium-tone blue topaz. For deep colored smalls, the market has been increasingly reliant on Africa. Today, in fact, many smaller stones sold in Brazil are African.

PRICED OUT OF REACH

Even if America had a change of heart with regard to expensive aqua, it is doubtful the supply situation for fine stones would improve. First of all, production of fine aqua is spotty. Secondly, the little fine aqua that is available has been priced out of reach of the American market.

Understandably, this domestic dearth of top aqua leads many to conclude it just isn't around. Not so. "It's just that many are gobbled up by Brazilian dealers for domestic consumption," says a San Diego gem

BRAZILIAN AQUAMARINE

cutter. According to this cutter, a specialist in Brazilian gems, the Japanese are also big buyers of the finer qualities—years ago in smaller sizes up to 5 carats but nowadays bigger sizes, too. "And," he says, "don't forget the Germans," an omnipresent force in the Brazilian gemstone market who take the complete gamut of aqua qualities.

Between Japanese and German aqua consumption, there isn't really too much of the fine stuff left to go around. What's left can cost U.S. jewelers an arm and a leg, especially if it's super-fine quality. Such stones are eye-clean, a necessity with pastel-color gems, and have robust shades of blue that are a far cry from the anemic aqua hues one sees in so much U.S. jewelry. "With stones so pale, it's no mystery why blue topaz has caught on so," the Brazilian gem expert says.

Nevertheless, there are some who think fine aqua is far too expensive relative to fine blue topaz. They assume that because Brazilian aqua is commonly heated, it should be as easy to produce fine aqua as it is irradiated blue topaz.

That's just not so. For while deep-color blue topaz can be produced almost at will, deep-color aqua can't and never has been. Heating is used to permanently remove common green overtones from stones—not deepen their color. Interestingly, similar green overtones in many African aquas cannot be removed by heating in ovens, a distinct advantage for the Brazilian variety. Yet even so, Brazil can't produce enough fine aqua to meet world demand. Dealers report finding increasingly more African stones in lots of so-called Brazilian goods. "Don't judge the world aqua market by sluggish U.S. demand," one importer cautions. "Once off our shores, the aqua market is ferocious."

CAT'S-EYE CHRYSOBERYL

Visit a fine Japanese jewelry store today and you will very likely see a selection of cat's-eye chrysoberyls sitting in the showcase reserved for men's merchandise. Demand is so great for this phenomenon gem in sizes up to 5 carats that nearly all the supply of better small cat's-eyes is being siphoned off to that Pacific citadel of prosperity. "Japan has a lock on the market," says one West Coast gem dealer.

Why the Japanese are so in love with cat's-eye is a bit of a mystery. It could be the translucent honey color. Or it could be the mysterious slit of reflected white light that intersects the stone lengthwise when cut in cabochon form.

Also a mystery: the gem's almost exclusive identification with men. As a result, cat's-eye is used mostly in rings, plus men's accessories such as cuff links or tie tacks. Dealers aren't really sure why this gem has such masculine appeal. They simply assume that cat's-eye chrysoberyl's "milk-and-honey" appearance lends itself more to men.

In this case, affluent men.

"There's just good and bad in cat's-eye," explains a San Diego gem cutter, "and nothing in between. What's more, the good is expensive— at least, in those 5-carat-plus sizes men in this country prefer."

Once above 3 carats, prices for fine to gem-grade cat's-eye climb rapidly—due to increasing rarity in larger sizes. For instance, a truly exceptional 3-carat stone might cost several thousand dollars per carat in a jewelry store. Its 10-carat counterpart might cost three times more per carat.

That leaves American men pretty much confined to the 4- to 6-carat-size range where increasing rarity, voracious Far East demand and non-stop dollar declines have pushed the cost to levels that force most prospective sellers to default from the market.

American jewelers have little choice. To spend less would mean downgrading to commercial qualities, an option most rule out (despite prices that are half or less than those of gem grade). Consequently, there isn't much of a market in commercial cat's-eye. Most consumers don't want to settle for less when it comes to this gem. It's easy to see why.

THE "EYES" HAVE IT

Fine cat's-eye must have a combination of elements—color, chatoyancy, clarity, translucency and proper cutting—to make it truly distinctive. Because so many factors come into play when judging cat's-eye, and so few stones measure up in the final run, the gem is usually found in high-end jewelry stores.

CAT'S-EYE CHRYSOBERYL

"You've got to develop a feel for cat's-eye," says a New York lapidary, "and that's not always easy given the relative scarcity of fine material and the out-of-the-ordinary criteria by which it is judged."

Unlike most gems, which depend on body color primarily to make it to connoisseur class, cat's-eye has got to excel in two areas: color and chatoyancy. Briefly, chatoyancy is a gemological special effect by which light reflected from very fine, densely packed rutile fibers is concentrated in a crisp line, reminiscent of the iris of a cat's eye, along the dome top of a stone when it is cut in cabochon form. Hence the name cat's-eye.

Obviously, the "eye" of such a stone depends on the hand of the cutter. If the cab is cut too flat, the eye will appear too wide, wavy and ill-defined. If cut too high, the eye might appear too thin. And if poorly proportioned, the eye may be off-center or run slightly diagonally instead of lengthwise.

In short, a good "eye" is one that is centered, sharp and straight—without being pencil-thin. Viewed on top under a single light source the eye should stay bright and defined as the stone is rotated in the hand. Ideally, the "eye" should be free of coloration from the stone's background. Often, however, there is bleed-through that gives the eye a yellowish or greenish cast, depending on which color predominates. Such interference is considered a drawback in connoisseur circles.

HONEY BROWN AND APPLE GREEN

After chatoyancy comes color. Cat's-eye runs a color range from raw honey-brown to apple green, with all sorts of mixtures in between. Although the men's market tilts strongly toward the rich yellow-browns, a slight hint of green is acceptable to some men while greener stones find favor with women.

"For the most part," one cutter says, "the honey colors come from Brazil, one of the two principal modern sources for cat's-eye chrysoberyl. The other source, Sri Lanka, tends to produce more of the apple-green variety. However, the Sri Lankan stones tend to have more defined and silvery 'eyes,' as well as greater luster."

Luster is related to both hardness (an admirable 8.5 on the Mohs scale, one of the highest for any gem) and translucency, the degree to which light penetrates a stone. Cat's-eye, also known as cymophane (from Greek words meaning to appear wave-like), should be neither opaque nor transparent. Opaque stones often lack the sensuousness of translucent stones while transparent and semi-transparent stones have overly watery color and dimmer, less defined "eyes." In a properly translucent

CAT'S-EYE CHRYSOBERYL

stone, says a Miami gem importer, "the eye shines sharply with either a slightly milky-blue or silvery cast."

When checking translucency also check clarity. This can be done, one dealer advises, by shining a penlight into the stone from the bottom to see just how included the dome may be. Lightly included stones are acceptable. Heavily included ones should be discounted or else disregarded.

Last, consider cutting. A stone should have a medium dome, one that is centered, not lopsided. When viewed from the top, the "eye" should run the entire length of the stone. "Some eyes give out three quarters of the way," a West Coast cutter says, "because the rutile fibers that make the eye just aren't there." When viewed from the side, the "eye" should appear to climb straight up the center of the stone from the base of its oval. One other thing: "Don't be afraid of bottom-heavy stones," the lapidary says. "You might think you are paying for needless weight. But the bottom adds depth to the appearance of both the stone's 'eye' and color."

One sure sign of a well-cut cat's-eye is what the trade calls the "milk-and-honey" effect. To observe this effect, shine a penlight on the stone's top from an angle instead of directly overhead. If cut properly, the dome will divide into perfect halves of light and dark, separated by the eye. In honey-colored stones, the "milk-and-honey" effect can often be quite spectacular as the half hit by the light turns a brilliant white and the half in dark turns a deep, burnished brown. But no matter what the color, if you hold the light stationary and rotate the stone, it will seem as if each half on the top is quickly passing from light into shadow and back into light again. Seeing such alternations of light and dark is one of the joys of cat's-eye ownership.

CITRINE

For years, citrine was to gems what muskrat still is to furs: so cheap and plentiful that no one took it seriously. A victim of its own common-ness, this earth-toned quartz only seemed to stir interest when, as often happens, it was confused with more expensive gems such as topaz, golden sapphire or even something as exotic as golden beryl.

Consumers may find it hard to understand how a gem could be reward-ed for abundance with neglect, but such was the case with citrine throughout the 1970s and most of the '80s. Now, suddenly, the gem's bargain price is no longer a handicap but an asset, especially to all those newly fashion-conscious jewelers who have learned from department stores just how well semiprecious stones attract increasingly important impulse dollars. Citrine has found favor with budget-minded women looking to expand their work and leisure jewelry wardrobes with affor-dable pieces that sport voguish earth colors.

And when it comes to providing earth colors for women on shoestring jewelry budgets, citrine has no real competition. Hues run the gamut from straw and sun yellow through clay orange to deep madeira red. In the past, it was the somberly beautiful madeira colors that were most prized. But with fashion colors tilted away from the hot and heavy to the light and lively, the action in citrine has moved to the vivid yellows and oranges that combine nicely with the aqua blue of topaz, the Life-Saver greens and pinks of tourmaline and the vibrant violet of amethyst.

Besides excelling at earth colors, citrine's low cost also makes it an ideal candidate for popular free-form fancy shapes (also known as "fan-tasy cuts"), very suitable for one-of-a-kind and customized jewelry pieces. As these highly individual stones captivate more consumers, citrine is sure to benefit.

The bottom line: a full-scale renaissance for this gem.

LESS IS BEST

Periodically, there have been design revolutions or movements in the jewelry field during which lavish use was made of all-but-forgotten col-ored stones, citrine in particular. Its low price allowed for use of very large stones with zestful colors that were extravagant but not vulgar.

Large citrines were set in many prized pieces from the Art Deco period between World Wars I and II, including the massive and elaborate Deco-inspired jewelry made for Hollywood stars like Greta Garbo and Joan Crawford in the mid- and late-1930s. Two decades later, citrines often appeared in David Webb's brilliantly eclectic trend-setting work.

Nowadays, however, the use of citrine has little to do with opulence

CITRINE

and luxury. Working women—not what David Webb once called "million-dollar ladies"—are the prime audience for colored stones, at least the affordable kind. As a result, low cost is high chic. As part of the trend, jewelry makers are using big, bold budget gems—many cut in a strikingly Cubist manner—to give lots of splash for little cash. At first, irradiated blue topaz and amethyst were the principal gems used. But once the market was saturated with these stones, jewelry manufacturers looked for alternates.

From then on, the rediscovery of citrine was inevitable. In fact, ever since the market was flooded with heated golden sapphire in early 1981, the jewelry world has thirsted for a very inexpensive earth-color gem. But designers always overlooked the most obvious candidate, citrine, instead experimenting with unattractive, low-end yellow topaz or hoping the public would pay the hefty extra for yellow sapphire. Neither was necessary.

Citrine, which dealers claimed was far inferior to yellow sapphire in terms of color and brilliance, owed its reputation more to extrinsic than intrinsic factors. "Who's going to go to the expense of cutting a citrine with the same tender loving care they would a sapphire?" asks a Beverly Hills dealer. Yet good cutting is as essential for citrine as sapphire. Unfortunately, because of its price, citrine usually gets second-class treatment from cutters. "Even the Germans, who are known for fine cutting, cut citrine with abbreviated faceting, using sandstone instead of the customary wheel," an expert in Brazilian stones concedes. "It's far cheaper."

In spite of cursory cutting, a lot of shapely citrines manage to find their way into the marketplace. And many of the best of them can still bring a hapless guess from jewelers that they are topaz, the other, far more coveted earth-color gem for which they have long been mistaken. Indeed, during the 1940s and '50s, citrine was routinely sold as topaz. Thankfully, taking gemology courses has taught many jewelers to tell the difference.

MADE IN BRAZIL

Citrine is the product of Brazil—both its mines and kilns. Essentially, citrines start life as either slightly smoky quartz or amethyst geodes. After heating, the smoky quartz turns clear and possesses a permanent color that is anywhere from light-yellow to medium-golden. Pop an amethyst geode in the same oven and the end result will be a brighter stone ranging in color from deep yellow to brownish red. Alas, these

CITRINE

more prized amethyst citrines rarely come in sizes above 3 carats. "If you see an 8-carat citrine," says one Brazilian gem expert, "it's invariably heated smoky quartz."

In the past, amethyst-derived citrine has been more favored. But with light yellow and golden colors more in fashion, smoky quartz citrine is easier to sell than formerly (as long as it isn't anemic and washed out). Presently, citrine sales are most active in calibrated sizes from 18x13mm down to 8x6mm (3-15 carats) in both emerald and oval shapes. "Jewelry manufacturers want the golden colors, not the pale yellows," a leading New York wholesaler notes. "They're matching them with stones like amethyst and pink tourmaline."

In any case, the once-prized wine-red madeira color is "out," so much so that fine citrine connoisseurs wonder why it was ever "in." "The madeira is over-burned and, as a result, too dull, too brown, too overpriced," one complains. "The orange-yellow stones have a lot more vitality."

Will golden citrine finally find a permanent place for itself in jewelry stores? Or will it suffer the same fate as the madeira citrine?

Many dealers lay odds that golden quartz, too, will be at the mercy of fashion cycles. Once a fad item always a fad item, they contend. And they cite the little respect this gem receives even in academic circles as proof of citrine's limited potential. For instance, the modern-day bible of gemology, Robert Webster's "Gems," pays token attention to citrine—only two short paragraphs in its 1,006 pages.

On the other hand, citrine's supporters believe esteem will improve if fantasy-cut, or sculpted, gems gain permanent acceptance. Labor-intensive free-form cutting forces reliance on abundant and affordable stones. With earth colors in vogue and citrine still one of the most inexpensive gems around, this golden quartz could be entering its long-overdue golden age.

CORAL

The natural pearl isn't the only worldwide casualty of pollution in the planet's seas. Now coral, the other great organic sea-gem, is in big trouble—at least in its finest, most coveted red colors. Just shop the major movers of coral in New York's Manhattan market.

At one importing company on 47th Street, the closest to pure red in coral is salmon-pink material. And because the current cost for decent red coral is so high, the firm doubts it will be buying premium grades any time soon. "The stuff is just not sellable at those prices," says a company principal.

Downtown the news isn't much better. "What you see is all we've had for months now," says a buyer for another Manhattan gem wholesaler, as she hands the firm's last three pieces of ox-blood coral to a visitor. "From now on, the industry will have to make do with hoarded goods or dribs and drabs of new stuff. But, basically, the sea is finished as a source of fine red coral."

This news jolts jewelers, used to seeing dealer booths at gem and trade shows brimming with coral beads, cabochons and carvings. The largess shouldn't fool them. "Most of what you see in coral today is lower grade, if it's natural," Crosby continues. "Worse, many strands and pieces that appear to be fine quality are very often dyed or made of reconstituted material."

Reconstituted? As in potato chips?

"As in turquoise or amber," the buyer corrects.

Whatever the case, a lot of coral sitting in jewelry counters is far less than meets the eye. The situation will only worsen if fine red coral becomes entirely a thing of the past.

ENDANGERED LIFE FORM

Highly treasured in ancient India, Persia and Rome, coral is nearly as much a mainstay of gemstone artisanry as amber and ivory, especially with American Indian craftsmen. As with other organic gems, coral was widely believed to have medicinal and mystical powers. Even today, coral powder is a popular aphrodisiac in India, which use prompts some gatherers to dynamite coral reefs. Such tactics, of course, only aggravate the fine-goods supply problem. But coral must fend off graver threats than TNT.

As a living organism, coral faces a slew of challenges to its survival, especially as the waters in which it lives become progressively contaminated. The creation process of the gem coral is peculiar and complicated. But, simply put, here's how it works:

CORAL

A multi-cellular animal called the coral polyp bands together in colonies with millions of its fellow polyps. For protection, each secretes a protective jacket for itself of pure calcium carbonate into which it retreats when threatened or not feeding. As the colony builds these shells, they couple together into branches and, if large enough, reefs.

Unfortunately, these calcium carbonate structures—which Gemological Institute of America chief gemologist John Koivula likens to "condominium complexes"—cannot withstand merciless predators such as the Crown of Thorns starfish which attach themselves to the colony and suck out all the lives. Often the polyps will abandon their homes when water conditions change for the worse. Whether ravaged or deserted, it is these coral skeletons (Koivula calls them "abandoned housing projects") that coral fishers process into beads, cabs and carvings.

Because coral is pure calcium carbonate, it is sensitive to chemicals, detergents, perfumes, even body acids which can eat away at it. That's why dealers and gemologists recommend periodic cleaning of coral in a mild soapy solution to rid it of all these abrasives. Even so, some softer corals, such as those from the Mediterranean, may need re-polishing every few years or so.

RED SALES IN THE SUNSET

Luckily, some corals are more resistant to chemicals and acids. The toughest, according to a Los Angeles coral specialist, come from the Sea of Japan, which is also the prime source of true ox-blood coral. "The Mediterranean produces red coral, too," he adds, "but it is not as hard as the material from Japanese waters."

In recent years, Taiwanese coral fishers have replaced the Italians—famous for centuries as coral carvers and cutters—as the main harvesters of this gem off Japan. But lately the Japanese fish and wildlife authorities have been enforcing strict coral quotas in the Sea of Japan and, as a result, sharply curtailing Chinese activity in these waters.

That leaves the Mediterranean which, long before the Japanese reined in on coral fishing, was so thoroughly fished and polluted that it was well on its way to becoming a lost cause for red coral. Not surprisingly, supplies of ox-blood and deep-red coral are dwindling sharply—despite exploration of farther depths for coral colonies. "A year ago, I had 8,000 to 9,000 carats of better to fine pears, ovals and rounds in red coral," Hagobian says. "Now I'm down to around 1,000 carats and having real difficulty getting back to old levels."

As dealer inventories of ox-blood and dark-red material disappear,

CORAL

prices to jewelers for these most-prized of coral colors soar. Consumers may be asked to pay a few thousand dollars today for a very fine 18-inch strand of 8-9mm ox-blood beads.

Deep red is not the only coral hue that appeals to connoisseurs. Many prefer the far-lighter blush-pink shades of coral, commonly called "angel skin." However, we did not find, as is often claimed, that prices for this lovely material exceed those of ox-blood. Although Tiffany is rumored to have paid a breathtaking $25,000 for a ring, earrings and 24-inch necklace ensemble of perfectly matched angel skin coral a couple of years ago, prices reported to us for top-grade angel skin cabs around 14x12mm were near but never as much as those of comparable-quality, dark-red material.

It goes without saying that the high cost of true red coral has invited rampant adulteration of this gem. Taiwanese and Hong Kong dealers, among others, are dyeing colorless to near-colorless material a reddish shade, one which dealers say is immediately distinguishable from natural-color coral. Worse, some processors are taking shivers and shavings of coral branches, combining them with a chemical binding agent, and selling the final reconstituted product as genuine coral.

So far, reconstituted coral is not as rampant as, say, reconstituted turquoise. But, some importers fear, it could become so if prices for red coral keep climbing. "I have no objection to 'pressed coral', or whatever you want to call it," says one, "but I just wish it would be sold as what it is—and not what it isn't."

AUSTRALIAN PINK DIAMOND

Call it either grace or irony. But scattered throughout western Australia's mammoth but so far mediocre diamond output, comprised mostly of industrials selling for under $10 per carat, are a few fancy pink stones that have commanded up to $400,000 per carat at auction. "We're talking pink with a capital 'P,' " says a New York fancy color diamond specialist.

Before 1985, few pink diamonds deserved even a small "p." So dealers settled for faintly colored stones, believing darker hues too much to expect from nature any more than once or twice in a century.

The discovery of diamonds in Australia gave diamond dealers new hopes. Although hearty pink diamonds from Down Under probably don't add up to more than a few thousand carats (in the rough!) of its 30-million-carat-plus annual production, this trickle is a flood when compared to output from Australia's past and present rival sources for fancy pink diamonds such as India, Brazil and South Africa. Indeed, some diamond people act like Australia is the first meaningful producer of true pinks.

This explains why the company that since 1982 has marketed the vast majority of Australia's diamonds, Argyle Diamond Sales Ltd., combs through its caratage with fine-tooth thoroughness, singling out the pinks for preferential treatment. As a result, few of these precious roughs wind up in the production Argyle sells to De Beers, its biggest customer, or even on the open market. Instead, the company cuts them in its own factory in Perth, then sells the very best of them at annual invitation-only auctions (called "tenders") in Geneva. At the third of these sales in November 1987, London jeweler Laurence Graf paid $3.5 million for all 30 lots—nearly double the $2 million aggregate of all the second-highest bids!

Given the dramatic sums that Argyle's pinks bring in behind-closed-door sales to dealers, it seems safe to conclude that trade professionals are convinced these covetables are likely to remain needles in huge haystacks—at best once-in-a-while rather than once-in-a-blue-moon affairs. What is it about Australian pinks that stirred up such a commotion in the first place?

BEYOND "PASTEL"

Argyle pinks possess sterling attributes, chief among them, deep body color. This attribute is no accident. Gemologist Stephen Hofer, Colored Diamond Laboratory Services, New York, one of the first to study Australian pink diamonds in depth, noted unique concentrations of minute

AUSTRALIAN PINK DIAMOND

pink grain lines inside Australian stones that were so dense they could not be told apart unless observed under extremely high magnification. While fancy color pinks from other localities also had pink grain lines, they were invariably fainter and sparser. Hofer therefore concluded that these grain-line congestions imparted very saturate color to Australian pinks.

No wonder, then, that a high percentage of Argyle pinks merit the distinction of being called "fancy" color. This is the Gemological Institute of America's highest grade for natural-color diamonds. Most non-Australian pinks submitted to GIA for grading rarely earned ratings above GIA's lower and bottom rung diamond color designations of "light" or "faint." A few managed to earn a second-best designation of "fancy light."

Yet during the first quarter of 1985, when dealers sent a total of 152 Australian pinks for GIA grading reports, nearly all earned the lab's top pink-color grade of "fancy." That's pretty astounding, considering the fact that those 152 pink diamonds represented more pinks, regardless of grade, than GIA ordinarily sees in a year.

We were fortunate enough to see several dozen of the first Australian pinks to arrive in New York. Their color struck us as indisputably "fancy." Never before had we seen such saturation of color in pink diamonds. One did not have to squint to see pink or use charitable euphemisms like "pastel pink" when talking about them. That's because many of these stones veer as much into the purple part of the spectrum as they do into what we call pink (a very desaturated form of red).

Along with the purple, however, often comes a large amount of brown and gray—resulting in a less-than-pure-pink color Hofer aptly describes as "smoky purplish pink." Use of the adjective "smoky" is meant to convey the impact of the color modifiers gray or brown, almost always present in Australian pinks. For some traditionalists used to fine pinks with color more reminiscent of raspberry, the presence of such modifiers is a drawback. Most dealers, however, think Australian pinks set their own, far superior standard of color excellence.

SMALL CHIPS OFF BIG BLOCKS

One of the only disappointments about Australia's big find of pink diamonds is their small size. Nearly all that we have seen are melee, averaging around 10 points. Yet, remarkably, the roughs from which these stones come are often fairly large. But due to their highly imperfect nature, as much as 90% must be cut away just to derive one decent polished stone. One dealer told us of a 2.5-carat rough that yielded only a

AUSTRALIAN PINK DIAMOND

31-point diamond. "And even this stone was still rejection," he adds.

Because most Australian pinks are small, and their color deep, their imperfections are generally more tolerable than if found in lighter color or white diamonds. Consumers with trained eyes might notice slight cracks or etching lines in some stones that impart a rough or pitted texture to small areas. Gemologists have taken to using the word "frosted" to describe the appearance of these areas.

Despite their size and clarity problems, Australian pinks have created a considerable commotion in a very short period. To us, they are truly admirable stones—so admirable, in fact, that the fuss made about them may encourage false expectations on the part of potential customers.

Sad to say, the saturate color common in small sizes is hard to find in larger stones. To date, we know of only one robust-pink diamond from Australia that weighed more than 3 carats, a 3.14-carat purplish-pink cushion-cut stone that sold for $1.3 million at Christie's New York in April 1989. Dealers worry that worldwide media attention paid to such a stone may result in a preference for dark pink—a preference that totally ignores the fact that this color is never found in larger stones.

But even if big pinks with deep color did come on the market with the regularity of small ones, few could afford to buy them. At the Christie's April auction, 16 Australian pinks were offered, ranging from 41 points to 3.14 carats. Of this group, 14 sold—10 of them to members of the public willing to pay tens of thousands of dollars for the privilege of owning pink diamonds with colors connoisseurs could only dream of a decade ago.

FANCY BLUE DIAMOND

These may be the worst of times, as far as supply goes, for natural-color (a.k.a. "fancy") blue diamonds. No one remembers it being quite so difficult to find fancy color diamonds with this much-coveted hue as it is now. And, worse, no one expects things to get better any time soon.

Oh sure, one can find stones with somewhat fanciful, rather than fancy, color that the Gemological Institute of America, this country's chief pedigreer of diamonds, compassionately classifies as "faint blue" or "very light blue." One may even locate stones with wishful tints that carry the lab's next highest rating, "light blue."

But just try to find true-blue stones that deserve any of GIA's really meaty grades: "fancy light blue," "fancy blue" or, on the rarest of occasions, "fancy dark blue." Here the pickings are the slimmest in decades. And auction prices, recently more than $200,000 per carat for a 4-carat "fancy blue" stone, reflect this nagging scarcity—and hunches that it will linger.

"It's been at least six months since we've had any blues in stock," says a New York fancy color diamond specialist. "If we had known that availability would become this much of a problem, we would have paid premiums on blues just to have them to show our customers."

Why is finding fancy-color blue diamonds proving so tough?

THE BLUE AS BAROMETER

Earlier in this decade, it was considered a truism that, except for one-in-a-million greens and reds, fancy pinks were the rarest of all natural-color diamonds. Then when Australia's gargantuan Argyle diamond deposits came on stream in the mid-1980s, miners unexpectedly found robust purplish pinks in something as close to abundance for this color as the gem world will probably ever know. As a result, blue has moved ahead of pink in the rarity rankings for fancy color diamonds.

Not that blue was terribly abundant to begin with. True, South African mines such as the famous Premier Mine had been known to produce this color—but never, it is believed, on the scale to which they were found in India's famed Golconda Mine, which operated for about 2,000 years, until 1725.

Nevertheless, South Africa could be counted on for blues—until, as a response to 1970s glut and 1980s recession in the fine diamond market, output at the Premier Mine was tucked in a bit. As part of the same iron-willed market stabilization effort, begun in 1982, De Beers withheld from distribution many of the most valuable roughs coming from its own mines or mines with which it was affiliated. That program was

FANCY BLUE DIAMOND

still in effect late in the decade. Cutters in New York and Antwerp sus-pected the embargo on top-grade roughs applied to both fine fancy colors and whites.

Withholding fancy colors would certainly be in De Beers' interests. For the past few years, the media has paid especially close attention to gem and jewelry auction results. Prices paid for fancy color diamonds—pinks and blues especially—are being taken as an indicator of the fine diamond market's overall health. This is why some dealers believe that De Beers is doing all it can to see that fancy colors perform well at auction, primarily reining in hard on supplies of the rough that yields them. "It doesn't take much to increase the scarcity of something that's already pretty scarce," notes another New York fancy color diamond specialist. "The Syndicate (short for De Beers in the trade) probably figures it's better that people make a big fuss over the price of a 1-carat blue than a 1-carat D-flawless diamond."

Of course, there is the possibility that De Beers, as omnipotent as it sometimes seems in diamond affairs, may have nothing to do with the present acute shortage in the American market of fancy blue diamonds. Instead, the steep slide of the U.S. dollar since September 1985 could have detoured many of the blues that once ordinarily came to the U.S. to more prosperous points of fancy color diamond popularity such as Japan, the Middle East and Europe. For instance, during a trip to Geneva in early 1989, this writer saw two spectacular fancy blues, the best he has ever seen, one a stone weighing just about 8 carats that had just been sold in a jewelry store for nearly $3 million. In mid-1989, the King of Saudi Arabia visited Switzerland with a gemstone shopping list that included a blue diamond or two.

"Fine fancy color diamonds in general have become as fashionable as fine art," explains a Shearson-Lehman broker who follows hard assets and collectibles. "There is still no end of 1980s new wealth waiting to convert a little of itself from its home currencies, however proud, to crème-de-la-crème tangibles such as Van Gogh paintings or high-provenance gems." The reasons? "Prestige and protection," the broker answers. "New money, like old money, seeks the sanctity of rare, prized possessions like fine-colored diamonds."

A DIFFERENT GLORY

The best blue diamonds have a beauty that is really not comparable to that of any other gem. Yet dealers constantly describe them in terms like "sky blue" or "satin blue" that imply a role model of other breeds.

FANCY BLUE DIAMOND

"If you're looking for something that has the rich midnight blue of a Sri Lankan sapphire, you'll be disappointed," says a fine gem dealer who sidelines in colored diamonds. "But if you're looking for a combination of moderate blue and unique brilliance, then the diamond has no peer."

Today such looking may take on the nature of a quest. Stones with exceptional hues are proportionately far rarer among diamonds than among sapphires. Usually, a dealer says, "the blue of a diamond is strongly modified by gray or black. Few stones have intense, saturate color."

This is a fact of life few jewelers are prepared for when they first stock blue diamonds. One possible reason: the 45.52-carat dark blue Hope diamond that dealer Harry Winston bought in 1947 and donated to the Smithsonian Institution 10 years later. The Hope has since become the most famous gem in America, perhaps the world. This stone's highly unusual inky blue may have encouraged unrealistic jeweler expectations. So when they finally encounter the norm of stones with strong intensity modifiers, they experience something of a let-down. "The trick is to learn to accept the blue diamond on its own terms," an importer explains.

Learning to do that requires a bit of an adjustment. But the extreme rarity of such stones really leaves no choice. What's more, minor color failings are generally compensated for by fire and brilliance, the diamond's two most celebrated virtues other than hardness. So it helps to incorporate the total criteria of diamond beauty into one's appreciation and evaluation of any fancy blue diamond. Admittedly, this takes some training.

However, since training requires experience, and the stones necessary for such experience are scarce, many dealers and jewelers rely heavily on GIA grading reports to form their judgment of stones. This can be dangerous. At best, GIA fancy-diamond reports are loose guides to color quantity—not quality. Because report grades represent very arbitrary cut-off points on a rather broad color saturation scale, even stones given the same grade can be vastly different. Therefore, nothing can replace the jeweler's own eye for a final verdict on the beauty of a blue diamond. "Make sure they face up blue," the importer says. "If they don't, they should be considered closer (in value) to white diamonds than fancy color diamonds."

FANCY BROWN DIAMOND

One fancy color diamond specialist I know likes nothing better than showing a mouth-watering array of lovely brown diamonds to out-of-town jewelers who visit him in New York. But the vacant stares that usually greet these stones quickly remind him that brown diamonds are still a seldom acquired taste. Nevertheless, he's convinced that some day soon the very same diamonds will become a required taste.

For reasons that have nothing to do with aesthetics.

"It's a matter of economics," he explains. "Fancy brown diamonds are just about the only bargains left in the diamond kingdom."

So it would seem. Today the standard pure-brown stone, possessing what the trade calls either coffee or chocolate color, costs no more than a commercial-grade colorless diamond in a 1 carat size—often far less. Indeed, side by side comparisons of the typical $2,000 to $3,000 colorless 1-carat retail store diamond with its same-price fancy brown counterpart will often show the brown diamond to be a far better bargain.

But it's a comparison few consumers ever get to make. When jewelers turn to brown, they nearly always use light cocoa or beige shades which, if mounted in yellow gold, pass for white at, of course, much less cost. Sad to say, brown is beautiful only when it can bluff as white.

At least with women.

But what about men?

"Men are a different story," my dealer-acquaintance insists. "Brown makes many men feel comfortable about wearing diamonds."

MALE AND MAJESTIC

Fancy brown or fancy color diamonds strongly modified by brown have long been favorites among diamond dealers who wish to wear diamond jewelry, rings especially. "The colors are so virile that a man can wear them and maintain his masculine image," the dealer explains. "Browns are ideal for the male ego."

If only more than a handful of males knew that.

The same earthen colors that turn many (not all) women off seem to turn men on when jewelers with savvy show them. Another fancy color diamond dealer wears a diamond wedding ring with a 1-carat brownish-orange emerald-cut stone, reminiscent of peak-color autumn foliage, that is among the most beautiful diamonds this writer has ever seen. Yet the cost to a consumer of a similar best-of-the-breed brown would be far less than that of the finest white 1-carat diamond—even though the brown stone is far rarer.

What keeps the price of beautiful browns low is lack of retailer

FANCY BROWN DIAMOND

appreciation, nothing else. Due to lack of interest, the roughs from which most decent fancy browns are cut still tend to be classified as industrial, a rating which makes them far less expensive than jewelry diamonds.

Nevertheless, De Beers—the diamond cartel which controls most of the world's diamond supply—is mindful of the fact that fine browns have been attracting more attention lately and so it has subjected the roughs that yield them to continuous price increases in the past few years. While this tactic has sometimes stimulated demand for colorless diamonds, it has so far failed to work with browns.

Many dealers don't expect the situation to change as long as men, the prime candidates for brown diamonds, remain such a tiny minority among diamond wearers.

"De Beers has targeted the men's market as the greatest growth area for diamond sales," says one dealer, "but the company is thinking only in terms of white."

But there's a ray of hope here. Given the average price for retail store diamonds these days, the term white is mostly a euphemism. Off-white is more like it. And once in the realm of off-white, you're really entering the realm of color, even if subtly. Admitting this fact of life could give brown diamonds—whose lighter shades of pale often face up far better than their more expensive yellowish-white counterparts—the opening they've long been looking for. In this case, familiarity might breed respect.

CALL ME COGNAC

For most jewelry diamonds, there are two continuums of color: yellow and brown. Yellows, known as the cape series, begin at colorless and browns at near-colorless, then both move gradually toward noticeable color density. The diamonds most jewelers sell fall into the cape category, which the Gemological Institute of America has quantified into a series of 23 progressively more yellow-tinged states represented by letter grades ranging from D to Z and keyed to use of master comparison stones.

Brown stones follow a parallel path of progressive color saturation. Only in the case of brown diamonds, stones rarely merit a color grade higher than H (what the trade calls "top light brown"). Once past J, and down to Z, many brown stones, as well as yellows, cross over into a limbo of sorts where they are graded either "faint" (roughly J to M), "very light" (N to R) or "light" (S to Z)—meaning they are neither colored nor colorless stones.

FANCY BROWN DIAMOND

When browns stones show enough body color looked at face-up to qualify as colored stones, they are eligible for one of three fancy color designations: "fancy light" (ginger ale colored), "fancy" (milk chocolate) or "fancy dark" (dark coffee). This latter designation is the end of the line for brown stones. However, yellows are permitted to go one stop beyond "fancy." When they do, they are deemed "fancy intense," a much more positive and popular term, says one dealer, than "fancy dark."

In any case, the term "fancy" before brown helps to reduce, often remove, the stigma of being brown. So does the visible presence of a secondary color, say yellow or, better yet, orange.

When buying fancy brown diamonds, remember that stones become increasingly expensive as brown is modified by other colors. Given all the possible color combinations, it is understandable that jewelers would seek out gemologists to help them describe color in diamonds. Gemologists record their findings on what are called diamond reports.

Grading reports from GIA, as well as its newest and strongest U.S rival, Colored Diamond Laboratory Services in New York, use very similar systems of verbal descriptions to reflect the degree to which brown is unmodified or modified by other colors. GIA and CDLS recognize six modifiers: yellow, orange, pink, red, green (called olive at CDLS) and black—any of which can be present in varying degrees.

To designate small amounts of modifying or secondary color (say roughly 1% to 25% of the stone's total color composition), GIA and CDLS use a suffix of "ish"—e.g., pinkish-brown. But once a modifier reaches approximately 30% to 40% of the color content, the suffix is dropped and the verbal color notation becomes pink-brown. Should pink account for more than 50% of the stone's color content, brown becomes the modifier and you have a diamond that gemologists will describe as brown pink. If the brown content drops to approximately 25% or less, the stone is called brownish-pink.

THE HOPE DIAMOND

Big, blue and fabulously fancy, the Hope Diamond is the most famous gem in the world.

The 45.52-carat stone, on display at the Smithsonian Institution in Washington, D.C., has everything going for it. The Hope is the largest deep-blue diamond in existence. It is steeped in mystery, with a lore as dark as its color. What's more, scientific study of the stone in recent years has added to the Hope's mystery and made it as much a legend with gemologists as it is with the jewelry-buying public.

For instance, the Hope is the only diamond of its kind to phosphoresce red—for reasons unknown. The stone's gemological prestige has been further heightened by the fact that it is an exceedingly rare Type IIb stone. Diamonds are classified either Type I or II, and within each category either a or b. The overwhelming majority of diamonds are Type Ia. Of those exceedingly few stones that are Type II, that is, nitrogen-free, most are a. Only a handful are Type IIb, a designation reserved for stones that are blue or grayish-blue.

But to merely call the Hope Diamond blue doesn't do full justice to its color. Experts rhapsodize about its indigo hue, and extol its red, green, purple and black highlights. However, says Susanne Steinem Patch, author of "Blue Mystery: The Story of the Hope Diamond," the gem's color is intensified by its blue-velvet museum display setting. "When unmounted, and viewed in daylight, it appears more of a sky-blue color," she says.

A RICH AND COLORFUL HISTORY

The Hope's history, prior to its purchase by its namesake, Henry Philip Hope, for roughly $90,000 in 1830, is as speculative as it is spectacular. To Patch, the Hope Diamond legend rests on an unproven 19th century theory—whose chief early advocate was London gem merchant Edwin W. Streeter—that the Hope was the largest of three stones cut from a famed parent stone, the French Blue, after it was stolen from the treasury of France in 1792.

If the theory is true, the Hope's origin is a magnificent 112.25-carat blue diamond found in the Golconda mines of India in the 1640s. The stone attracted the attention of Frenchman Jean Baptiste Tavernier, the greatest gem dealer of his day, who acquired it on one of his Indian journeys. Tavernier sold the stone for 220,000 livres (about $45,000) in 1668 to Louis XIV, king of France, who, later unhappy with its irregular shape and lack of brilliance, ordered it recut by the court lapidary in 1673. When finished, the stone weighed 67⅛ carats, more than 45 carats

THE HOPE DIAMOND

less, and was triangular shaped. It became known as the Blue Diamond of the Crown, the prize of the French Crown Jewels.

Sometime during the reign of Louis XIV, the dark stone started to take on associations with dark forces. Supposedly one of Louis' mistresses, Madame de Montespan, fell out of favor with the king and was banished from the court after she wore it. Patch suggests a cause other than a diamond curse for the ruler's disaffection: Madame's implication in some poisoning scandals.

Yet Hope legend lovers cling to that story as a precursor of the bad luck future wearers would have. Two kings later, when Louis XVI and his famous wife Marie Antoinette were guillotined, the Hope curse is said to have been in full force.

In any case, it is at this time that the fabled stone ended its career as the French Blue. When the French Revolution broke out in 1792, the Blue Diamond was stolen with many other Crown Jewels. It was never again seen in the form in which it disappeared. Instead, it is believed to have been cleaved into three stones, the largest of which, a 45.52-carat cushion, surfaced in London during the early 1800s.

In 1830, a London jeweler Daniel Eliason sold this cushion to Lord Henry Philip Hope, a British banker (whose company helped finance the Louisiana Purchase) and gem collector. Henceforth it was known as the Hope Diamond. To give some idea of the mystique that by then surrounded the stone, we quote from the entry for it found in an 1839 catalog Hope had prepared by Bram Hertz for his entire gem collection: ". . . . in vain do we search for any record of a gem which can, in point of curiosity, beauty, and perfection, be compared with this blue brilliant."

The diamond passed on to Hope's nephew and then, in 1887, to the nephew's grandson, Lord Francis Hope, a gambler and black sheep of the family. As luck (or the curse) would have it, Lord Hope squandered his fortune and was forced to live off the earnings of his American wife, May Yohe, an actress. To meet the expenses of his extravagant lifestyle, Hope tried for years to get permission to sell the gem but was prevented from doing so by his brother and three sisters. In 1901, a year after his wife ran off with an American sea captain and left Hope penniless, he finally sold the diamond for a never-disclosed sum. However, the new owner, New York diamond dealer Simon Frankel, declared its value to U.S. Customs at $141,032, then paid a 10% duty on the sum. It took Frankel seven years to finally sell the stone, in Paris, to a collector named Habib. A year later Habib sold it to two French diamond dealers, Auroc and Rosenau, who bought it as partners.

THE HOPE DIAMOND

THE HOPE IN AMERICA

In 1911, Pierre Cartier obtained the stone, reset it, and sold it to Evalyn Walsh McLean, of Washington, D.C., wife of the owner of *The Washington Post*. The price: just under $180,000, payable in monthly installments.

McLean was both fascinated by and fearful of the diamond's reputed dark past and reportedly had the stone blessed by a priest. Proud of her acquisition, she talked up its legends for all they were worth at Washington cocktail parties. That, if you believe in curses, was asking for trouble. Sure enough, McLean's first son was killed at the age of 9 in an auto crash. Her husband became so infatuated with another woman he became an incurable alcoholic and eventually died in a mental hospital. Last, her daughter committed suicide at age 25.

McLean died in 1947. The Hope then passed to New York diamond dealer Harry Winston, who purchased McLean's jewelry from the estate for $1 million. Winston kept the diamond for 10 years, using it to raise money for worthy causes by displaying it at benefits. In 1958, Winston donated the stone to the Smithsonian (in return, it is said, for a 10-year tax write-off). The museum received several protests from groups and individuals who warned that accepting the stone would bring the same bad luck to the nation as it had its previous owners.

Since its donation to the Smithsonian, the Hope Diamond has become the most famous gem in America and the world. Given such lofty stature, it is hardly surprising that the stone has finally begun to arouse a bit of a critical backlash. After more than 300 years of nearly unanimous acclaim as an aesthetic marvel, the Hope now has many detractors who find it fancy to a fault—and accuse it of being too steely, inky or dark. But the stone's admirers, still the majority among experts, would no doubt agree with one fancy-color diamond specialist who praises the stone for being "every bit as beautiful as its reputation leads one to expect."

THE TIFFANY DIAMOND

Looked at with no regard for its 100-year history, the Tiffany diamond is, according to experts who have studied it closely, the following: a bulkily cut square antique stone weighing 128.51 carats, borderline fancy light to fancy yellow and VS, not flawless clarity as most texts state. Seen in this light, purely as a diamond with no past, these experts estimate its present value at $1 million.

Yet as an historic stone, the same experts say the diamond could probably command $5 million today.

This jump in value is due to the Tiffany name. The diamond's worth stems far more from a glorious history than from gemological glory.

"Frankly, the Tiffany diamond isn't all that remarkable," one of the appraisers who puts its worth if sold privately at $5 million says somewhat clinically. "Because it is cut so thickly, it looks much smaller— around 80 carats—than it actually is. Further, the color is nothing to rave about." Then his manner changes abruptly. "But factor in provenance and we are talking about another stone entirely."

A MATTER OF MYSTIQUE

A generation ago, when standards for fancy color diamonds were less strict, the Tiffany diamond was accorded a stature many versed in colored diamonds feel it no longer merits. These dealers object to the almost promotional descriptions of the stone, often found in trade and gemological literature as, among other things, the largest and finest canary or golden diamond known. Unfortunately, writers continue to take these accolades at face value rather than at arm's length.

Nowadays, however, a good many experts believe the Tiffany diamond deserves fame far more as a marketing marvel than a natural wonder. That's probably as it should be, suggests one jewelry historian, given the fact that the store's founder, Charles Tiffany, often cited the influence of P.T. Barnum for much of his success. Certainly, the Tiffany diamond testifies to the power of provenance in establishing the reputation and worth of many gems and pieces of jewelry. By provenance we mean the careful documentation of a gem's background or origin (sometimes both) and any consequent prestige conferred by such credentials.

This isn't meant to debunk the Tiffany diamond. To the contrary, every diamond dealer we know who has inspected the stone finds it attractive. But these same people all agree they would have paid far less attention to the stone if it didn't reek with a century of mystique. Seen from the perspective of provenance, the Tiffany diamond easily ranks among the most distinguished stones in history. In terms of American

THE TIFFANY DIAMOND

history, in fact, it is second only to the 45.52-carat Hope blue diamond on permanent exhibition at the Smithsonian Institution in Washington, D.C. No wonder there are some who believe this stone, like the Hope diamond, should be considered a national treasure.

FROM CAPE TO CANARY

Ironically, the stone spent its first 15 years at Tiffany largely unheralded before being taken from wraps to rapture. Jewelry historian Mary Murphy Hammid, an appraiser with Christie's auction house in Los Angeles, notes that no mention is made of the stone in either the first or second editions of Edwin Streeter's important book "The Great Diamonds of the World," published in 1881 and 1882 respectively. Why Tiffany hesitated to capitalize on the stone is a bit of mystery. Eminent gemologist George Kunz, then a Tiffany vice president, is said to have authorized its cutting in Paris during 1878 only after a year of planning—and then under his personal supervision.

Because he had it cut in a square shape, with 90 instead of the usual 58 facets, some historians, seconded by diamond dealers, believe Kunz was shooting for maximum strength of color—as opposed to fire—when viewed through the top. The trouble was, say experts, there wasn't that deep a color to begin with. "It's definitely classifiable as 'fancy' but not 'fancy intense' color," says one fancy diamond specialist. Hardly surprising then that when the rough (eventually sold to Tiffany for $18,000) that yielded the diamond was found at South Africa's famous Kimberley Mine in 1877, it was considered important mostly for its size, not its color. If anything, fancy yellow diamonds had become somewhat common after the first major South African diamond strike in 1867. A decade later, the country was a well-known producer of yellow diamonds, many of them huge. Consumers will do well to remember that the term "cape," a pejorative trade term for yellow, comes from South Africa. In time, of course, the trade substituted the far more euphonious term "canary" for many of the yellow stones it sold to the public. This may be why the Tiffany diamond is so often called a canary stone. But experts say the term "canary" should only be used for a few select stones that are intensely colored, something the Tiffany diamond isn't.

THE PRIDE OF CHICAGO

Tiffany first unveiled its 128-carat behemoth at the Chicago World's Fair in 1893, noting in its special guidebook to the event, "It's not only the largest diamond in this country but is heavier by 23 and three-eighths

THE TIFFANY DIAMOND

carats than the well-known Koh-i-noor diamond." When Tiffany showed its diamond again at the Pan American Exposition of 1901 it was still ballyhooed as the largest diamond in America.

By the time of the 1933-34 World's Fair, again held in Chicago, the stone had solidified its status as one of the world's best-known fancy color diamonds. According to Hammid's painstaking research, the Tiffany diamond and the 42-carat bluish Emperor Maximilian stone were selected to represent the world of fancy colors at a $5 million diamond display that included a simulation of a South African diamond mine complete, the fair's guidebook proclaimed, "with native laborers." The diamond also took feature billing at the 1939-40 New York World's Fair. In 1957, for, most appropriately, the Tiffany Ball in Newport, R.I., the stone was first set in a piece of jewelry—in this case, a necklace worn by Mrs. Sheldon Whitehouse, the event's chairwoman.

At present, the Tiffany diamond sits alone in a special glass showcase across from the store's diamond counter, mounted on a stem that extends out perpendicularly from the wall and bathed in strong yellow light to heighten its golden color. A 1971 book, "The Tiffany Touch," says the stone is the store's stellar attraction, a statement that holds true today and most likely will for as long as the stone is on display.

FANCY YELLOW DIAMOND

The stone that kicked off South Africa's diamond rush in 1868 was a 21-carat yellow rough that was later cut into a 10.73-carat oval cushion called the "Eureka." This find would have seemed to augur great things for the world supply of colored diamonds, especially those of the yellow variety, which until then had been as rare as any other color.

Fate had nothing that grandiose in mind. Instead, South Africa merely swelled the number of what the trade has ever since called "cape" (after South Africa's Cape of Good Hope) diamonds. These are stones whose yellow content is generally not considered a plus. But when the yellow was sufficient to give the diamond an identity as a full-fledged colored stone, it was deemed "canary." Today, such diamonds are more apt to be called "fancy yellow."

However, it must be stressed that very few diamonds merit the designation of fancy yellow—or fancy color of any sort.

"I doubt that there are ever more than 4,000 carats of fancy color diamonds over 1 carat available to consumers worldwide in any given year," says one New York specialist in these goods.

Yet the fact that fine fancy yellow diamonds are far scarcer than fine whites does not seem to have much impressed the jewelry buying public. In 1989, when fancy color diamonds had become the darlings of connoisseurs worldwide, top-notch yellows were still not all that more expensive than top-notch white goods—despite their greater rarity.

Why haven't consumers flocked to these bargains?

THE SECOND TIME AROUND

Fancy-color diamonds rarely attract novice buyers. One specialist in these goods says tradition, which associates the diamond with the attribute of brilliance rather than color, calls for a buyer's first stone to be colorless. However, he adds, "The second time around, many diamond purchasers tend to be far more indulgent and far less traditional, thus opening the way for sales of fancy color diamonds."

Maybe so. But few jewelers explore the customer's subsequent openness to fancy colors. This is a pity because the same money spent for a medium, but not fine, quality 1-carat colorless diamond can also buy a decent fancy yellow stone.

Obviously, it takes more than affordability to make consumers feel comfortable buying fancy color diamonds. It also takes getting used to thinking of diamonds as colored stones. That's something even jewelers find hard to do.

FANCY YELLOW DIAMOND

SHOW ME YOUR PAPERS

The term "fancy" covers a broad spectrum of hues and saturations. This is especially true for fancy yellow stones. Pure-yellow fancy diamonds stretch in saturation from straw through lemon to taxicab yellow. Yet the Gemological Institute of America, the school that gave the trade its grading systems for both white and fancy color diamonds, merely subdivides the yellow range into three loose categories—fancy light, fancy and fancy intense—on its popular diamond grading reports, often used as pedigrees by jewelers. Fancy color diamond experts rail against reliance on these reports because they feel GIA's color grades are woefully vague. It's easy to see why.

In 1987, Stephen Hofer, a gemologist who founded Colored Diamond Laboratory Services, New York, ran color strength (saturation) analyses of several hundred yellow diamonds using an electronic colorimeter. His tests revealed a gamut of color strengths that is at least three times greater than that covered by GIA's 23-grade D-to-Z damond color scale—in use for decades with colorless-to-cape stones.

Therefore, to color grade fancy yellow diamonds with the same precision as colorless ones would require a 69-grade scale—at least in theory. Such a scale is impossible in actual practice because the GIA's method of color grading is based on the use of comparison diamonds, known in the trade as "master stones." Fancy yellow stones are too varied, and their cost too prohibitive, to regularly assemble master stones sets with even five diamonds (the number in most colorless-to-cape stone sets), let alone 69. Nevertheless, lumping fancy yellow diamonds, whose color array far outstretches that of conventional diamonds, into three rather spacious color categories clearly does them a disservice.

To make matters more complicated, many fancy yellow diamonds possess traces of secondary color: brown, green and orange. While these secondary colors merit a mention as modifiers on GIA fancy color diamond reports, these documents fail to give any meaningful idea of the modifier's strength. All that is done is to distinguish weak from strong modifiers by using the suffix "ish" (as in brownish) when the secondary color is less than 25% of the overall hue. If more than 25%, the suffix is dropped. Critics of the GIA's fancy color diamond reports say they are too limited to help consumers make comparisons between stones and therefore must be used only as general guides.

A KNACK FOR NUANCE

While GIA fancy color diamond reports have their drawbacks, they have

FANCY YELLOW DIAMOND

at least begun to curb the rampant abuse of characterizing all yellow diamonds, whether faintly or fiercely colored, as "canary" stones. Originally meant to convey strong yellow color, the term "canary" degenerated into a catchall description for any diamond that appeared yellow (as opposed to yellow-tinged) when viewed through its top. With the advent of diamond grading, the term has been narrowed to mean extremely saturate pure-yellow or orangish-yellow stones that fall into the GIA category known as "fancy intense." It goes without saying that true canary diamonds are rare and expensive.

Thankfully, yellow diamonds don't have to be canary (in the modern sense) to be lovely. Medium yellows, as well as strong yellows modified by brown (the least valuable secondary color for a diamond), present some of the biggest diamond bargains around. But to get the most beauty for your money, consider buying a shape other than the familiar round brilliant—most likely a marquise, pear, oval, or "radiant" cut. (These last have bottoms cut like rounds but tops which are square, rectangular or cushion.)

Why are round brilliants usually not as desirable when buying fancy yellow diamonds? Because this shape maximizes brilliance and, in the process, washes out all but the strongest color. This doesn't mean that fancy color stones should lack the fire for which diamonds are prized.

Fine cutting, the key to diamond dazzle, is as much a virtue with colored as with colorless stones. One way to tell how well a marquise-, oval- or pear-shaped fancy color diamond has been cut is to study the hourglass-like zone of color washout (called a "bow tie") in the center. The smaller and less distinct the bow tie, the better the cutting job. If you are considering a modified cushion, or "radiant" cut, watch out for stones cut so thick—in order to retain weight and color—that they seem dull and lusterless.

When considering a fancy yellow stone, ask whether or not it possesses the common diamond characteristic of blue fluorescence (a tendency to emit blue color when struck by ultraviolet rays, a strong component of sunlight and other light sources). While this ultraviolet-excited blue increases white in colorless diamonds, it will, if moderate to strong, reduce the amount of yellow in fancy color stones. How? Fluorescence changes the stone's light-absorption properties, muting yellow to various degrees. On the other hand, yellow fluorescence—a far rarer phenomenon than the blue variety—adds sizzle to the color of fancy yellows.

COLOMBIAN EMERALD

There he was, standing in his undershorts and shirt, in a small, private office at the Miami airport that seemed, under the circumstances, as big and as public as Grand Central Station. The Florida gem dealer, an emerald specialist, had just returned from a routine buying trip to Colombia, the world's leading producer of this green beryl.

But emerald wasn't what the six customs agents were looking for in the linings of his luggage and clothes that spring day in 1981. They were looking for cocaine, the estimated $16-billion-a-year cash crop that is Colombia's No. 1 export. After a fruitless 90-minute search, the agents told the dealer to get dressed and go home.

Such are the hazards of life for Americans nowadays in the Colombian emerald trade, a trade closely linked in the minds of many to that country's wild and woolly drug trade. Rightly so. Ever since the United States and Colombia began their abortive joint campaign against drug trafficking in 1983, these hazards have increased. At first, reported *The Economist*, Colombia's powerful cocaine community tried to stop the crackdown by offering to deposit $5 billion with the country's central bank to boost its sagging foreign-exchange reserves—in return for immunity from extradition. When the government declined, the drug dealers declared open season on U.S. officials, killing scores of DEA (Drug Enforcement Agency) operatives before forcing America to call off its hounds.

Meanwhile Colombia's rich and powerful drug lords evidently set their sights on a takeover of the country's flourishing emerald trade, murdering hundreds of miners and dealers who stood in their way. In February 1989, a major emerald miner, Alberto Molino, was gunned down, along with 11 bodyguards and 16 guests, at a party he was giving. No wonder American gem dealers feel a distinct sense of gangland menace these days in Colombia. "The mines were already dangerous, but now Bogota's no longer safe either," says one New York emerald importer. Even the Florida emerald specialist, a fearless and frequent traveler to Colombia, postpones trips there until absolutely necessary.

But even without threats to their safety, American dealers would have had strong reasons to stay away from Colombia. The free fall of the U.S. dollar against the Japanese yen since September 1985 has given the Japanese—inveterate lovers of Colombian emerald—their greatest buying leverage since the 1970s. Tokyo dealers flocked to Bogota, driving up emerald prices, in U.S. dollar terms, as much as 75% in less than two years and much more since—while scarcely feeling the increases in their own ballooning currency.

COLOMBIAN EMERALD

THE RIVAL GREENS

With prices for Colombian emerald their most breathtaking ever, American jewelry makers and retailers have taken refuge in less expensive goods from Zambia and Brazil. But the Japanese will have little to do with these varieties. Why?

Put a row of fine Colombian emeralds next to rival-grade stones from its nearest competitor, Zambia, and dealers will invariably choose the Colombian stones as the finest. Partly because of their vanadium content, the Zambian stones seem to possess black or gray which the Colombian stones, colored instead by chromium, lack.

But just because fine Colombian emerald enjoys supremacy among connoisseurs doesn't mean this variety enjoys the same market leadership in the market's middle and low end. In America, Colombia's superior green is no longer enough to command the manufacturer and retailer loyalty it did a decade ago. Cutting, clarity and cost are equally important factors now. And it is in these three areas that Colombian emerald took a beating during the early and middle 1980s, largely due to Colombia's hide-bound refusal to meet the challenge of new competition.

That challenge comes from Israel and India, the two main cutting centers for non-Colombian emerald. In 1976, Israel jolted the emerald world by introducing superbly cut, often strikingly clean African emerald in unheard-of calibrated sizes and fancy shapes. To gain market share, the Israelis strongly undercut prevailing market prices. This combination eventually wore down market resistance to the new emerald.

By 1982, Zambian emerald had stolen the top-commercial and medium-quality sectors away from Colombia. Then supplies of African emerald temporarily dried up (exports from Israel dropped from a record high of $65 million to around $20 million in 1984). During the lull in Zambian production, Colombia responded to Israeli savvy with some long-overdue savvy of its own.

First, it began to cut its prices. This move wasn't entirely altruistic, however, having much to do with over-production and the strength of the U.S. dollar between 1981 and 1985. Dealers knew that dollar gains would quickly compensate them for selling at rock-bottom prices. So between 1982 and 1985, Colombian emerald prices were slashed at least 30%. (They've since shot back to historic highs.)

Second, Colombians realized that the highly included emerald common in years past was no longer salable in the United States. So they offered far cleaner goods, some of it (like the material from Buena Vista) as brilliant and clean as that from Zambia (albeit often lighter toned).

COLOMBIAN EMERALD

Even goods from the famed Muzo mine seemed to boast greater cleanliness.

Third, cutters in Bogota began to improve their cutting by importing Brazilians to teach them better makes and new shapes. Nevertheless, cutting is one area where Colombia still seeks to improve its reputation.

THE ENEMY WITHIN

Once, if ever, cutting in Bogota is on a par with that in Tel Aviv, U.S. dealers will have only one other beef with Colombia: the country itself. Forget that Bogota of the 1980s makes Chicago of the 1920s seem like Winesburg, Ohio. Red tape and bribery, norms of doing business in nearly any Third World gem-producing country, set new standards in Colombia. Here's why.

Around 1975, the government leased emerald deposit sites for five years to private entrepreneurs who proceeded to rape the land. It took nearly a decade to get rid of the ensuing glut. To prevent such surfeit again, the government has closely regulated mining, even halting production entirely for months at a time. Dealers do not find restrictive governmental control the solution to rapacious private mining. "There is a growing amount of bureaucracy in Colombia that makes doing business there needlessly complex and unpleasant," one importer says.

But in a country with more than one-third of its 28 million people unemployed, bureaucracy itself has become a major form of employment. Since most of these bureaucrats are peasants who come from backgrounds of extreme poverty, relations between them and affluent American dealers are often touchy and temperamental.

Ultimately, dealers hope, the Colombian emerald market will normalize, especially as farm commodity prices, so important to Colombia, pull out of their current deflationary tailspin. "Then peasants can return to agriculture and get out of the emerald business," a dealer says. Don't bet on it. With emerald the No. 1 seller among traditional colored gems worldwide, and fine Colombian emerald the choice of connoisseurs everywhere, it will be harder than ever to keep the country's peasants down on the farm.

ZAMBIAN EMERALD

Jewelers are finding it harder than ever to make a plus of emerald's greatest minus: its tendency to be highly included. The old ploy of calling the numerous wisps and veils of commercial Brazilian and Colombian stones something exotic like "jardins" (gardens) falls flat nowadays.

What killed the acceptability of emeralds whose insides look like exploded cotton balls?

Blame it on Zambia, the African country where in 1976 geologists discovered a radically different kind of emerald (a gem whose name is derived from the Greek word, smaragdus, for green) than that known for centuries. Roughs yielded stones so clean that dealers at first suspected they were synthetic, with their stark, saturate greens that looked almost ominous next to Colombian stones with softer, sweeter hues.

The contrast between the two triggered an immediate clash in the marketplace. At first, establishment dealers resisted the new material, but gradually viewed it, somewhat condescendingly, as a cheap alternative to high-priced Colombian goods. It took a group of intransigent outsiders, some from Israel and Afghanistan, to make the no-apologies-needed case for the new-breed beryl. In time, their devotion to it earned Zambian emerald parity with Colombian goods. Indeed, in June 1989, Tiffany's began advertising Zambian emeralds per se.

But winning over jewelry stores like Tiffany's took time. Even some of the staunchest supporters of the African emerald harbored secret doubts about its aesthetic parity with Colombian material. Until only a few years ago, says one African emerald specialist, "I sold Zambian but preferred Colombian goods." So it was with other secret doubters.

Because Zambian emerald has fostered radically higher expectations about mainstream emerald, ones that stones from other localities find it harder to meet, this material now has a strategic importance to the market, especially in its broad middle echelons. Indeed, when Zambian production faltered badly between 1982 and 1986, the entire emerald market suffered. It is probably no accident that the current boom in emerald sales coincides with a return to production levels in Zambia during 1987 that recalled the days of plenty back in 1980.

FROM EBB TO FLOW

Until March of 1987, supplies of decent Zambian emerald, especially light and lively, medium-to-better 1- to 2-carat goods had been growing steadily scarcer. In fact, as of January of that year, New York's main importers of African emerald were seriously worried about the future of Zambia's deposits. One of them had even switched from emeralds to diamonds.

ZAMBIAN EMERALD

Then, in February 1987, word came from Israel that there would be significant quantities of decent-to-top-grade Zambian stones available once again. "Production has resumed in Zambia," an Israeli dealer told us then. "Maybe it's not as great as it was in 1980, but it's enough to calm market fears." Actually, this dealer underestimated the flow of goods. Eventually, the market would see a return to old output levels.

But why had supply of Zambian emerald become so sparse in the first place? Cutters in Israel attribute the dearth to politics. As one dealer there put it rather delicately in 1986: "Zambia has been concentrating on taking control of mining." To do this, it had to eliminate a powerful entrenched network of smugglers whose leaders operated out of Geneva, Switzerland. After jailing hundreds of suspected gem poachers and shooting at least eight of the most prominent contraband dealers, Zambia launched its own rough distribution company.

Although its stepped-up surveillance of mine areas failed to eliminate smugglers, the Zambian government's full-court press against them brought it enough rough to launch periodic state-run auctions, the first of which was held in November 1985. Material from this and subsequent auctions, most of it cut in Israel and India, flowed into the U.S. market until the Zambians suspended these sales and embarked on a bold new venture.

In January 1988, the government decided there would be more profit to itself if it cut as much of the rough it was buying as possible. So it opened a 200-man cutting factory in Ndola whose entire output, averaging 5,000 carats a month, is sold exclusively to a Swiss company based in Zurich.

THE CLAMOR FOR CLEAN

Despite the resumption of supplies from Zambia, shortages in the early and mid-1980s were so great that dealers still have a fingers-crossed attitude about the future. Their fears are understandable. We hate to contemplate the effects of another drought in supplies of this stone, which has had as profound an impact upon emerald aesthetics as did the introduction of Colombian material into Europe several hundred years ago.

While the ideal for color in emerald is still debatable (Colombian green still has the edge with connoisseurs), Zambian stones have allowed the jewelry market to savor aesthetic qualities never before associated with emerald, at least not man-on-the-street goods.

Today, with decent 1-carat emerald the most expensive it has ever been, consumers are entitled to great expectations about the emeralds they

ZAMBIAN EMERALD

are buying. As a result, they will no longer put up with fissure-ridden stones the way they had to in the past. True, fissures that reach the surface of stones have for centuries been routinely oiled (with everything from resins to, more recently, polymers) to hide these tiny cracks. But since this oil is not necessarily permanent and stones sometimes revert to their pre-beautified condition, the idea now is to offer consumers emeralds that need minimal oiling and preferably none at all.

Zambia is the first emerald producer to give consumers who cannot spend the enormous sums charged for fine emerald a chance to buy unoiled stones on a regular basis. The reason: Because Zambian stones tend to be cleaner, proportionately fewer take to oiling even if subjected to it (cracks must break the surface of stones for oil to penetrate).

But greater cleanliness is only one virtue. Stones tend to be more brilliant—so much so that they lend themselves to a diamond cutter's philosophy of brilliant beauty. As a result, jewelry makers and retailers can reject the highly included staple stones they once had to sell in favor of stones with the same kind of crisp, clean appearance they're used to seeing in diamonds.

It is no accident that dealers in Israel, long a major diamond cutting power, were the first to exploit the higher luster of Zambian emeralds. Using precision cutting techniques of a standard far above those applied to emerald elsewhere, the Israelis were able to make as big a name for themselves in the colored stone world as they had in the diamond world—in a far shorter time.

Not only did the Israelis cut for maximum brilliance and beauty, they introduced emerald in a wide range of fancy shapes and offered them in calibrated sizes unavailable anywhere else. The Israeli approach to emerald cutting worked so well that it is being imitated by the Brazilian cutters who currently man Zambia's state-owned cutting works. "The Israelis set a standard that spoiled the market," says one New York dealer. "Now everyone expects you to equal them."

DEMANTOID GARNET

Twenty-eight years after it was discovered in 1868, gemology pioneer Max Bauer wrote that demantoid garnet would probably never earn full-fledged gem status. Much as he admired the stone, Bauer thought it was too small, soft and scarce to merit anything more than curiosity.

Just about the same time, the late 19th century's other great gemology pioneer, George Kunz, was in the Ural Mountains of Russia, demantoid's prime source, buying every piece of demantoid rough he could find. Kunz, on leave from Tiffany's where he served as the store's chief gem buyer, was financed by banker/tycoon J. Pierpont Morgan, an avid gem collector.

For more than a decade, Kunz had been a devotee of the Russian green garnet, so much so that Tiffany's made more extensive use of the gem than any other jewelry store of the age. Indeed, demantoid was as closely associated with Tiffany's in the late 19th century as tsavorite, a distant-relative green grossular garnet discovered 100 years after demantoid in East Africa, is with Tiffany's in the late 20th century. True, demantoid was a darling of upper crust English and French jewelers. But the gem owes much of its popularity with connoisseurs today to the Tiffany mystique—despite the fact that it has been at least 65 years since the last significant production of Ural Mountain demantoid.

Thanks to Kunz, demantoid achieved, and still retains, an importance far disproportionate to its availability. "Maybe one in every 10,000 pieces of Victorian jewelry used demantoid," says jewelry historian Joseph Gill. "Yet you'd never think how little of it there actually was with all the fuss they make about it today."

Why the big fuss? The gem's name gives a clue to the cognoscenti's lingering love.

DISPERSION GREATER THAN DIAMOND

Almost all garnets are plagued by very low dispersion (light refraction). But demantoid, a member of the andradite family, is an exception, blessed with more of this attribute than even diamond, a stone prized for its dispersion. No wonder, then, that the garnet's first sellers named it demantoid (meaning diamond-like), after the Dutch word "demant" for diamond. (In case you're wondering why marketers used a Dutch word, keep in mind that Amsterdam was still the world's principal diamond-cutting center at the time the garnet first came on the market.)

The new garnet's fiery brilliance gave the stone, usually found in small sizes, a decided edge over lesser-luster emerald and peridot, the period's leading jewelry-use green gems. Indeed, Gill says, demantoid was often

DEMANTOID GARNET

sold as "olivene" or "Uralian emerald." That is why many pieces of Victorian gemstone jewelry made between 1885 and 1915 feature demantoid. In fact, the stone is almost wholly identified with the Victorian era.

Luckily for demantoid, America and England had fallen under the heavy spell of Darwin-inspired naturalism. The resulting fascination with brute nature was manifested in jewelry design as a voguish use of bird, fish, flower and reptile motifs. Since green symbolized nature, jewelers gravitated toward emerald. However, motif pieces consisted largely of melee and, as said earlier, demantoid was the green melee stone of choice among the knowledgeable.

No doubt, larger demantoids would have figured as prominently in late 19th century jewelry, only supply prevented it. The stone was extremely rare in sizes over 2 carats. The largest specimen we were able to see when researching this article was a magnificent 8-carat stone in the private collection of a New York dealer.

THE TELLTALE INCLUSION

Demantoid garnet is probably the only gem whose inclusions are considered an aesthetic property, as important as color and brilliance. Believe it or not, the value of a stone depends heavily on the prominence and definition of what are called "horse-tail" inclusions (bundles of byssolite—a form of asbestos—that spray out in a curve from a central chromite crystal).

Although a few yellowish-green garnets containing horse tails have been found in the Italian Alps, this happens so infrequently that most gem dealers still consider the horse tail to be, in effect, a Ural Mountain birthmark. "Technically speaking, the horse tail isn't conclusive proof of Russian origin," warns one gemologist. "It's just a very good indicator. To be absolutely sure, you'd have to do chemical analyses."

Consumers may wonder why such ado is made over finding one particular type of inclusion in the first place. Does it really matter if a demantoid is from Russia? The answer is yes. A large part of demantoid's mystique, historians note, is its Ural heritage. Since these mountains also produced small amounts of alexandrite, emerald and pink topaz, the best of which are said to be paragons of these species, Ural mountain gems have a prestige based on locality.

This doesn't mean that a horse-tail is all that matters when buying demantoid. But its presence certainly helps to distinguish stones from horse-tail-free ones found in Czechoslovakia, Arizona and, more recently, Mexico—as well as the majority of stones from Italy. Another diffference

DEMANTOID GARNET

is color. Most non-Russian stones are so yellow (the result of coloring by iron as opposed to chromium) that they should perhaps be called topazolite, a greenish-yellow andradite.

DEMANTOID VS. TSAVORITE

The only real competition to demantoid, color-wise, is tsavorite, a green grossular garnet found, so far, only in East Africa. To traditionalists, this newer-find garnet is far inferior to Ural Mountain demantoid. But a newer generation finds tsavorite as praiseworthy as demantoid.

The preference battle resembles that currently raging between fanciers of Colombian versus those of Zambian emerald. Fine demantoid garnets, like fine Colombian emeralds, tend to have a sweeter, livelier color, with preferred tones a bit lighter than those of their African counterparts. But the greater gravity of tsavorite color, like that of African emerald, has become much less of a drawback to acceptance.

Where tsavorite has a clear edge over demantoid is in hardness (7 on the Mohs scale for tsavorite, 6½ for demantoid). That half-point difference may not seem like much, but it translates into a decided durability edge for tsavorite. This helps explain the preponderance of garnet brooches and pins in estate jewelry. Demantoid's softness made it unwise for use in rings. The lack of large sizes also contributed to a paucity of demantoid ring stones.

At present, demantoid is basically a collector stone with a very small following outside this circle. Several times in the last few years, we have seen fine demantoids that had been bought at flea markets for a song because unsuspecting owners had no idea of their identity or value. "If you buy an old piece with bright green stones in it," advises Gill, "don't dismiss them as peridots or tourmalines. If demantoid, the value of the piece could jump considerably."

MALAYA GARNET

Nearly 20 years ago, some miners in East Africa went looking for a purplish-pink garnet called rhodolite which was very popular in Japan. One day, while digging for rhodolite, the miners found a strange orange and sometimes reddish-orange garnet mixed in with the pink garnet.

"What is this stuff?" one asked.

"I don't know. But whatever it is, no one will want it," another answered.

And, sure enough, the Japanese kept rejecting this new garnet when offered it by dealers in Nairobi, Kenya. In time, the African dealers came to treat the gem with contempt.

Gradually, as miners kept finding more of this nuisance gem, they nicknamed it "malaya," a Swahili word that means, first, "outcast," and, second, "prostitute"—but connoting, above all, trash. They called it malaya because dealers soon told them to stop bringing this new gem to them.

Then, in the late 1970s, some Americans (and Germans, too) happened to notice the orange garnet and began questioning the African dealers about it. "Oh, you mean the malaya," the dealers would say, a bit surprised.

"What's malaya?" the Americans would ask.

"It's a misfit garnet that no one has any use for," the dealers invariably replied.

"But it's beautiful," the Americans would insist, and buy some to sell to collectors back home.

In no time at all, the new garnet had garnered a small but passionate following among gem collectors, principally in America. And prices for top grades quickly flew to levels that left the Nairobi trade aghast. Then when gemologists declared the gem a completely distinct breed of garnet, prices for top stones were on the wing again.

Today, despite greatly slackened demand, fine malaya still commands nearly what it did when it took the American market by storm in 1979.

The point of the anecdote is this: One man's garnet is another's gold. Especially when it comes from East Africa where garnet breaks all the rules.

PLAYING PYGMALION

Although malaya is no longer considered an outcast or misfit gem, the name still sums up the gemologist's frustration with this garnet, much as it once did the dealer's. Malaya is a mongrel garnet—part grossular, pyrope, almandine and spessartite. Some gemologists have already labeled it part of a garnet group called pyralspite to convey that it is

MALAYA GARNET

basically a cross between pyrope, almandine and spessartite.

Visually, malaya most often resembles spessartite and hessonite, two brownish-orange to orange garnets that are as rare as this newer species. Nevertheless, the idea of paying prices for these garnets that are 10 to 20 times what they are for garden variety red, pink and purple garnets is something most jewelers refuse to do—rarity be damned!

Jewelers aren't alone in their hostility to malaya prices. Some dealers stubbornly maintain that the malaya market is a hoax and that no garnet, except extremely rare and much-coveted demantoid and tsavorite, is worthy of connoisseur prices. For these dealers, the word "garnet" still conjures five-and-dime birthstones and class ring pyropes.

But to gem collectors and connoisseurs, the main audience by far for malaya, the new garnet has earned full respectability. It may even be fair to say that malaya is the most respected non-green garnet—outside of exceedingly rare true rhododendron-color rhodolite and some of the more remarkable of the color-change garnets coming out of East Africa.

In recognition of malaya's new stature, some prim and proper Europeans are trying to play Pygmalion and have the name changed to "umbalite," after the Umba Valley region of adjoining Kenya and Tanzania where the new garnet is found. But American dealers won't hear of it. "The name 'umbalite' is nowhere near as euphonious as 'malaya,' " says a major marketer of this gem.

Instead, he urges the industry to stick with the stone's original name, just the way it has with "tanzanite," the trade name for a zoisite that is also found only in East Africa. "Malaya is such a beautiful-sounding word," the malaya maven continues, "that the trade will stay with the word, even if the species nomenclature is changed to umbalite."

Meanwhile, the Europeans continue to tinker with the malaya name. "Leave well enough alone," urges a Tanzanian dealer. "The name is a great selling point."

SUNKIST COLOR

Although malaya resembles other garnets, the best of the breed have a distinctive pure-orange color. In fact, one stone importer jokes that most true-color malayas should come stamped "Sunkist" because their color is exactly that of a California orange.

Occasionally, however, malayas possess a beautiful pinkish orange which dealers aptly describe as "peach." Due to the rarity of these peach-colored stones, prices for them in 5- to 10-carat sizes are higher than the pure-orange variety when they are clean and well cut.

MALAYA GARNET

On the other hand, stones with a dash of red go for a little less. Mix in a bit of brown with the orange and prices for malaya garnet become as down to earth as their color. At present, dealer stocks of true malaya garnet are more than ample, particularly in Idar-Oberstein, Germany's renowned colored stone cutting center, which is famous for African gems. This is good news because mining of malaya is at an all-time low in East Africa, still this gem's only known source.

One last note: Consumers should be aware that thousands of carats of junky brown garnet were sold to countless gem investors as "malaya" in the early 1980s. We have seen so-called investment gem portfolios that featured these reject stones. It is even possible that some jewelers have been shown these garnets by investors anxious to unload them. If that was your jeweler's first experience with malaya, chances are it was probably his or her last. So you might have your jeweler look at the marvelous 14-carat stone photographed for this essay to dispel earlier impressions of this gem. Rest assured, those ugly brown garnets that investors bought are not malayas—not even low-grade ones.

"It is a shame that many people including jewelers were exposed to imposter malaya," says a West Coast dealer who was one of the first to import this garnet to America. "If so, they should give this beautiful gem a second chance. That's what the Africans who named it malaya in the first place did—and their change of attitude made them money."

RHODOLITE GARNET

Is it possible for a gem species identified with class rings to have class?

For years, serious respect has eluded red-family garnets due to their association with school colors and signet jewelry.

Now newer strains of red-family garnet, found mostly in East Africa and Sri Lanka, are bringing long-overdue stature to the stone. These strains are called rhodolite garnet and feature, at their best, a lovely vibrant violet, often reminiscent of an orchid.

For the last 20 years or so, ever since rhodolite was found in abundance in East Africa, nearly 50% of all these garnets that have made their way to market in 1- to 5-carat sizes exhibit strong purples and pinks. Of this number, a good many possess prized purple-pink "day-glow" shades that rival similar hues found in tourmaline and fancy sapphire.

"Contrary to popular opinion, rhodolite is not necessarily a deep-toned, overly saturated red or purplish red," says a West Coast importer. "In sizes under 5 carats especially, many stones show lighter tones and less saturated colors."

It is these lighter pink and purple rhodolites that are stealing some thunder away from rubellite. And no wonder. Prices for fine rhodolite in sizes up to 5 carats are very often one quarter those for kindred-color rubellite. Eventually, that could give this tourmaline some difficulty once the word is out about rhodolite, especially since rubellite tends to be far more included than garnet.

What's more, rhodolite inclusions are generally too fine to be readily seen by the naked eye. Instead, stones take on a velvety appearance (although a promising new deposit in Tanzania is producing cranberry-color stones that are noticeably devoid of this slight sleepiness in appearance).

"Sometimes you'll find slight bubbles and silk, usually in the fabulous purples," says a California miner and jeweler. "Reds tend to be flawless and water-clear." For the most part, however, rhodolite presents jewelers with a very affordable gem whose color, clarity and brilliance are second to none. "It's just a matter of breaking down popular misconceptions about the stone," a dealer adds.

PYROPE'S PURPLE COUSIN

The term "rhodolite" dates from 1898 when it was first proposed as a descriptive term for some newly discovered, rhododendron-color garnets found in North Carolina (hence the name "rhodolite"). In his landmark gemological treatise, "Precious Stones," Max Bauer classified this "rose-red to purple" stone as an "intermediary between pyrope and alman-

RHODOLITE GARNET

dine" garnet. It has remained on the books as such ever since.

Then, and now, pyrope (usually blackish red) and almandine (usually brownish red) have been the far more entrenched jewelry stones, continuously overshadowing this newer garnet group member. Only recently, within the last 10 years, has rhodolite begun to make a name for itself.

Alas, the grouping with pyrope and almandine has carried with it a false but lasting impression that rhodolite, like its brethren garnet, is over-dark—although admirers like Bauer told the world it wasn't so as early as 1903. Because it has not yet established a reputation for itself, "The gem is one of the most undervalued in the world," says Bauer's modern-day counterpart, Dr. Frederick H. Pough.

Given its very low price and its great availability in fine colors, the obscurity of rhodolite makes no sense. Thankfully, rhodolite is finding a wider audience. The Japanese have been big enthusiasts for more than a decade and the Chinese in Hong Kong have begun to follow their lead. If the past is any guide, West will meet East in terms of a fully developed taste for rhodolite—first and foremost in America, where gem bargains are most appreciated.

Already, notes one dealer, "My sales of rhodolite are running nearly neck-and-neck with amethyst, and you know how big a seller amethyst is." Others are even afraid that rhodolite will catch on so fast that demand will quickly outpace supply. "I have orders from manufacturers for fine-color pink-purple rhodolites that I am finding difficult to fill," one explains.

SMALL IS BEAUTIFUL

At present, there are two principal sources for purplish-red rhodolite: Sri Lanka, India's island neighbor to the south, and East Africa. In addition, lighter, less saturate pink garnets, which some believe shouldn't be called rhodolite at all, are coming from India, often at a fraction of the price of the East African variety. For classic pure-violet rhodolite colors, however, jewelers will have to turn to Sri Lanka, according to the miner/retailer. But this preference will mean spending more money. "The stones' greater cost in Sri Lanka may explain why more dealers mention Kenya as their prime source for rhodolite," he says. A recent find in Tanzania is also responsible for a sudden availability of less expensive rhodolite.

Nonetheless, "expensive" is a fairly relative term when used in connection with rhodolite. Unlike fine aquamarine, rhodolite doesn't need body mass to bring out its best color. Indeed, 1-carat stones often show

ZIRCON

A diamond by any other name is a zircon. Or it was for a couple of centuries, one of them ours. Since the mid-1970s, however, a diamond by any other name is more likely to be cubic zirconia.

Due to the name similarity, many jewelers assume that zircon, a natural diamond substitute, and cubic zirconia, a manmade diamond simulant, are one and the same—or closely related.

They're not.

But the widespread belief that they are stymies efforts on the part of zircon zealots to improve the much-maligned reputation of this gem. Many devotees protest the backhanded treatment zircon, the December birthstone, receives.

Yet zircon isn't the first gem to find its birthstone status more a hindrance than a help. Reflect for a moment on spinel, a gem in chronic low standing with those legions of jewelers who refuse to believe it anything but a cheap mass-production synthetic. And the fact that a large number of antiquity's finest and rarest "rubies" have been identified as natural spinel doesn't seem to change matters.

So it goes with some birthstones. The irony of all this is that zircon enjoys a rather formidable status among gem collectors. Indeed, like corundum and tourmaline, the gem comes in a wide enough variety of colors—blue, green, yellow, orange, red and brown—to make collecting it a specialty in itself. "I know that half the zircons I sell to jewelers will never make it to their showcases," says a Beverly Hills gem dealer and zircon enthusiast. "They're buying the stones to keep for themselves."

THE STIGMA STORY

To be sure, such jewelers are few in number. The Beverly Hills dealer estimates that he has sold no more than a dozen zircons in the last year or so. "None of them were colorless," he adds. "Anybody familiar with zircon knows that other gems do a much better job of imitating diamond."

That evidently wasn't the case a century or two ago, perhaps more, when gem dealers discovered that heating cinnamon-color zircons often made them permanently colorless, more brilliant and, well, highly reminiscent of you-know-what. From then on, the gem was largely but not entirely thought of as a poor man's diamond, although for years the trade disguised the pretender status for these cooked-to-colorless stones by calling them "Matura diamonds" in honor (or dishonor) of the place in Sri Lanka where they were mostly found. (Nowadays, far more jewelry-grade zircons are found in Southeast Asia, particularly Thailand and Cambodia.)

ZIRCON

Not all in the trade looked down on zircon. To his everlasting credit, eminent 19th century gemologist George Kunz, for years a Tiffany's vice president and its main gem buyer, proposed marketing zircon as "starlite" (a tribute to its highly refractive nature) around the turn of the century. Although this name was short-lived, it represents the most notable attempt at positive thinking about zircon ever launched in the gem trade.

Kunz was right to celebrate zircon. The gem is practically its own rainbow—even without application of heat treatment. Nevertheless, this form of color alchemy is responsible for the chief zircon varieties—colorless, blue and gold—that have been used in jewelry.

With such a wide palette of color to offer, zircon has managed to withstand the diamond substitute stigma. But it has never dealt that stigma a crushing blow, even though its name is derived from the Arabic word *zargun*, meaning "gold color," evidently a tribute by the ancients to its generally reddish-brown color state when found in nature.

BEYOND BLUE

Strangely enough, many of the relative few who think of zircon only as a colored stone, not a diamond look-alike, still fail to do this gem full justice. Dealers who stock zircon in depth tell us that at least 80% of their zircon sales are in one color: blue. This blue is one often reminiscent of gray-tinged African and Indian aquamarine, even "London-blue" irradiated topaz. Occasionally, stones are said to verge on sapphire blue.

Because it comes in such pleasing blue shades, it is easy to understand why blue zircon was used frequently in Victorian jewelry, especially in the 1880s. Indeed, Victorian jewelry is one of the principal sources of large zircons over 5 carats nowadays. "When I'm in England," says the British-born Beverly Hills dealer, "I often see zircon jewelry in fine antique shops. Invariably the stones are blue."

Given the preponderance of blue zircon in the better antique zircon jewelry that he sees, the dealer suspects that many of the calls he gets for blue zircons are based on the need for replacement stones for estate pieces.

BRILLIANT BUT BRITTLE

Consumers considering zircon should know about some of this gem's characteristics. Those who have seen secondhand jewelry with zircon in it probably know this stone is brittle. That is usually evident from abraded facet junctures, a problem easily remedied by re-polishing.

ZIRCON

However, to hold future wear and tear of zircons to a minimum, keep stones out of rings and instead put them in brooches, pendants, earrings and pins. By the way, earth-tone zircons are ideal for men's tie tacks, stick pins and other dress-up jewelry.

Besides brittleness, many unheated zircons possess a cloudy or smoky appearance that may, if too pronounced, be a minus. Interestingly, however, smoky pale-gray zircons were once commonly used in "mourning" jewelry.

In zircon's favor is its great brilliance and dispersion (fire), near enough to diamond, as said before, to fool the unaided eye. Fortunately, zircon is doubly refractive and diamond singly refractive. So it's easy for a gemologically trained jeweler to tell the two apart if questions arise.

To take fullest advantage of zircon's great luster, stones are usually cut into rounds, albeit modified ones with an additional set of pavilion facets. But among zircon specialists and connoisseurs, emerald shapes seem more highly prized. The reason? "You'll know when you see one," the Beverly Hills dealer answers.

RHODOLITE GARNET

off the stone to best advantage. It is larger rhodolites—over 10 carats—that tend to darken up and show more red.

"Over 10 carats, it becomes increasingly hard to find rhodolites with that fantastic violet," the jeweler says. By 15 to 20 carats, the per-carat prices of stones with fine orchid colors can be 10 times the price of small pieces. Price is purely a reflection of rarity.

Fortunately, demand for rhodolite has been concentrated in smaller sizes, enabling many retailers to stock a full inventory for very little money. In fact, a jeweler could display a wide array of rhodolite in sizes from 1 to 5 carats for the same money that it would cost him to buy a single medium-grade 1-carat ruby or a very fine rubellite. Abundance, plus still-slack demand, is keeping rhodolite's price way down. So jewelers who want to stock colored stones in depth, yet invest relatively little money, can increasingly be expected to stock this garnet. Rhodolite seems destined to beat the same path to success as aqua, blue topaz and amethyst.

"Purple, pinks and violets have become such hot fashion colors in recent years that more jewelry manufacturers than ever are using stones with these colors," a West Coast importer explains. "No stone gives these colors with such clarity and brilliance as rhodolite. And when you tell people its cost, the stone is even more of a turn-on."

INDICOLITE

With the price of fine sapphire climbing to new heights in the late 1980s, the search is on for replacement blues. One gem that some dealers mention as a sapphire substitute is indicolite, a member of the tourmaline group whose name comes from indigo but whose finest colors more often suggest the menthol blue of topaz than the denim-to-dusky blues of corundum.

This isn't to say that indicolite can't pass for sapphire. It's just that we've seen tanzanite and iolite do a better job of standing in for this gem. Nevertheless, the high price of fine sapphire has definitely opened doors for indicolite. Once of interest primarily to collectors, the stone has begun to find a following among jewelry buyers, principally in Switzerland, Germany and Japan.

There are several reasons why affluent jewelry shoppers are attracted to this tourmaline—reasons that we think have as much to do with spending smart as dressing smart. Buyers of indicolite are evidently drawn as much to its rarity as its beauty. Like it or not, a subtle undercurrent of, dare we say it, investment is creeping into the international fine jewelry market—more so in Europe and Asia than in America—that makes indicolite a logical jewelry gem option.

Integral to selling indicolite are the facts that its mineral-gel blue rivals that of the very brightest "London blue" irradiated topaz while being far, far scarcer and all-natural to boot. It will never be a mass-market stone, nor do its buyers want it to be. They like its elitist stature and its, as yet, non-elitist cost. The price of a top-grade 5-carat indicolite should seem a steal compared to that of an above average, if not quite fine, sapphire of the same size—even though the stone is far rarer.

TOUCHES OF GREEN
Despite the 1988 discovery of two sizeable pockets of this gem in Brazil, these finds probably didn't swell world supply by more than 12,000 carats in terms of finished goods. We're talking here of true-blue indicolite—not the greenish-blue tourmaline that is often pawned off as it.

Seeing true-blue indicolite is practically a once-in-a-lifetime experience for most jewelers and probably most dealers. One Seattle gem importer who always tries to have indicolite on hand says that less than 10% of what is offered to him as this gem fills the bill. In 1988, that was fewer than 20 stones, all under 8 carats. The vast majority of the indicolites shown to him had perceptible shadings of green. Other dealers report the same low ratio of acceptable stones from those sent or shown them.

The high number of reject indicolites raises a question of major con-

INDICOLITE

cern to consumers: Does the presence of visible green nullify a tourmaline's right to be called indicolite? Nearly every dealer to whom we asked this question took a hard line on the issue, insisting that no trace of green whatsoever should be tolerated.

If that's the case, finding true indicolote might take some time. Of the stones given us to examine, a good many had too much green to warrant the name indicolite. In others, the green was quite subordinate to the blue, present only enough to be characterized as something akin to a very pleasant teal color. The dealer who showed these latter stones to us was adamant about their right to be called indicolite. "If slight amounts of green disqualify a tourmaline as indicolite, there will be almost no stones dealers can sell as this gem," he said.

That so many indicolites are greenish makes perfect sense since they frequently occur in pockets of green tourmaline. When they do, they usually account for less than 1% of the material found. Because the term indicolite is basically descriptive and often highly subjective, many mineralogists are uncomfortable with it. One who has done extensive research on tourmaline, Pete Dunn of the Smithsonian Institution in Washington, D.C., ridicules the term indicolite as a "trivial varietal name."

Whether called indicolite or not, the sight of true-blue tourmaline is still cause for celebration among connoisseurs of this gem group—one that boasts a very wide color range. "Now that irradiation is being used so successfully to create pure red tourmalines, pure blue has become the rarest tourmaline color," says one tourmaline specialist. So it is hardly surprising that this dealer remembers the spine-tingling day he was offered four "ravishing" pure-blue African indicolites cut from the same crystal. "I knew I had to have them," he recounts. "It took a couple of years, but eventually I got them." The best of the four—one the dealer refuses to sell and, instead, keeps in his own private collection—is the marvelous 21.14-carat specimen pictured at the opening of this chapter.

Adding to the rarity of this stone is its African origin. Although indicolites have been reported from Mozambique, Madagascar and Nigeria, it is Brazil that has always been this stone's chief source by far—with Maine ranked a very distant second. In fact, when in 1903 the gemologist Max Bauer wrote the last revision of his magnum opus, "Precious Stones," Africa wasn't anywhere on his list of sources for indicolite. However, Russia and India were. Interestingly, indicolites were found in the same Kashmir district of the Himalayas that produced the world's best-ever blue sapphire.

INDICOLITE

"BRAZILIAN SAPPHIRE"

It is perhaps ironic that indicolites were found mixed in with sapphire, for this tourmaline has often been mistaken for blue corundum—so much so that it was once known as "Brazilian sapphire." The confusion with sapphire helps to explain the name indicolite, which is, to the best of our knowledge, an alternate spelling of "indigolite," a color-based name this tourmaline went under many years ago.

Unfortunately, say those familiar with indicolites that resemble sapphire, the comparison is generally not flattering. According to the tourmaline specialist, these indicolites are highly reminiscent of the overly dark sapphire from Australia.

The reason sapphire-like indicolites are so blackish blue, the dealer explains, is cutting. Tourmaline exhibits the most marked dichroism (change of color when viewed in different crystal directions) of any gem. Therefore, the choice of cutting axis (called orienting) will strongly influence the stone's color and transparency. If cut along the wrong axis, stones darken to the point of becoming muddy and opaque. Judging from the stones we looked at while preparing this essay, cutters nowadays have got the hang of orienting indicolite. But while they seemed to have learned how to make stones look as transparent and bright as aqua, they have not found a way to hide green. All except a few were varyingly greenish, some objectionably so.

Given the wide variation in indicolite color, it is doubtful this gem would prove endearing to any but one-of-a-kind jewelry manufacturers, especially when the market has become so used to irradiated blue topaz, a stone known for its almost eerie paint-chip-color consistency from one stone to the next. Color sameness is hardly a complaint we hear uttered about indicolite. To the contrary, when dealers are asked for custom blendings of this gem they often have to tell clients to wait a bit. Indicolites are extremely difficult to match for pairs and suites. So if you are lucky enough to find such a grouping, expect to be charged a 20% to 30% premium for the trouble it took to assemble it.

IOLITE

When tanzanite, a baked-to-blue zoisite from East Africa, took the jewelry world by storm in 1969, Tiffany's, its main marketer, didn't exactly give the gem away. Yet by 1980, the newcomer was considered the poor man's sapphire. However, with prices of very fine tanzanites often $1,000 per carat and more in retail stores, this gem has been elevated, as far as being a substitute, from the poor man's to the yuppie's sapphire. Consequently, jewelers are on the prowl for a new poor man's sapphire.

They won't have to look far or long for the next great bargain in blue. A relatively plentiful gem found in India, Sri Lanka, Tanzania, Zimbabwe and, most recently, Brazil has been waiting on standby for more than two decades to play just this stand-in role.

It's called iolite. And many jewelry designers who watched irradiated blue topaz become the aquamarine substitute of the 1980s are betting that iolite will become the sapphire substitute of the 1990s.

Certainly, its price is right, if not always its hue. Stones up to 5 carats usually don't command more than $100 per carat in retail stores while the price of sizes between 5 and 10 carats rarely exceeds $150 per carat—ceilings that most likely wouldn't change much even with a sudden surge in demand.

Why? Iolite, say dealers who stock it, just isn't cut out to be an expensive gem.

PLEOCHROIC TO A FAULT

Iolite (the name comes from *ios* the Greek word for violet) is commonly known as "water sapphire," an apt description because its color very often lacks depth and density. One reason for its thin color is the fact that iolite, like its fellow blue bloods, sapphire and tanzanite, is pleochroic—meaning it transmits light differently when viewed from different directions to the crystal. Only in the case of iolite, the pleochroism is so acute that it is almost an affliction.

Ironically, the Vikings made iolite's pleochroism a virtue by using thin slices of this stone as a light polarizer. Believe it or not, iolite will do exactly what a camera's polaroid filter will do: cancel out haze, mist and clouds to make things appear clearer. By observing the sky through iolite, Viking navigators were able to locate the exact position of the sun on overcast days. Where, you might ask, did these famous seafarers get iolite? Well, it's been found in, among other Viking haunts, Greenland and Norway.

But the moderns have yet to learn from the Vikings. Iolite still confounds aesthetes with its strong pleochroic stops and starts of color. For

IOLITE

instance, an iolite cube shown us for this article was a sweet violet blue on one side, then gray white on the next. Its color literally disappeared, then reappeared, as the cube was rotated from side to side. For this reason, iolite is also called dichroite. Actually, the name is wrong since this species is trichroic. But while the name "trichroite" may be more accurate, it is no less derogatory.

Dealers convinced of iolite's merits, and their number is growing, blame cutters for making the gem's pleochroism so problematic.

"You cut this stone the slightest bit off axis and you will flat-out destroy the color," says a Seattle gem importer. "But cut it right and this stone will stand up to comparison with fine sapphire. In fact, I'll bet you that many jewelers at first mistake it for sapphire."

But for iolites to earn the supreme flattery of mistaken identity with fine sapphire, they have to have good color in the first place. Not too many have such color. In fact, iolites are often cursed with an ink-spot blue that makes them overly dark. Big deal, you say, so are many sapphires.

In the case of sapphire, however, stones lend themselves to color correction by heating in ovens while iolites cannot be cooked to lighten color. Nature pretty much has the last word when it comes to iolite color. It also has the last word when it comes to iolite clarity—another big difference between it and sapphire, which can be heated to remove milky rutile. Thankfully, stones with good color but poor clarity can be cut in cabochon form, a common fate for iolites. However, there seems to be enough stones with decent color and clarity to support a modest market in faceted iolite.

THE TIME IS NOW

Actually, there already is something of a market in iolite, one that consumers may not even be aware of—even those who buy this gem. That's because their iolite usually comes in multi-color rainbow gem jewelry where it serves almost exclusively as a sapphire substitute. Iolite is plentiful and cheap in the tiny calibrated sizes needed for these pieces. And while most jewelers will make it a point to tell customers that the blue sapphire-like stones in these rainbow bracelets and necklaces are really iolites, it's not a name that readily sticks in the memory.

But now that iolite is being used as a solo or feature stone in more jewelry, name recognition is on the rise. Indeed, iolite is mentioned more and more by designers concerned about the rapid rise of sapphire prices in the Far East during the past few years.

IOLITE

What's holding back significant usage is the general lack of familiarity with the gem. Some specialists in esoteric stones report a flurry of inquiries about iolite—usually regarding its price, availability and durability. While their answers to the first two questions are comforting, they cannot be as reassuring about the gem's toughness.

Relative to sapphire (hardness: a 9 on the 10-point Mohs scale), iolite (hardness: 7 to 7½) is far less durable. But relative to tanzanite (hardness: 6½), iolite will probably hold up a little better. In any case, neither iolite nor tanzanite is advised for rings that are to be worn every day or fairly often. If set in earrings, pendants and the like, there should be no problems as long as pieces are spared abuse.

Although mining of fine iolite is spotty, there has been considerable accumulation, in Germany especially, of high-grade iolite over the past 25 years—enough to support use of it on a broad basis for some time to come. Unquestionably, German dealers in Idar-Oberstein are the kingpins of the iolite market because they began amassing this gem long before anyone else did. Even today, the Germans are the most active and avid buyers of iolite rough in the world. "They knew that eventually this gem would find a place in jewelry stores," says one U.S. dealer. "Now they're about to cash in."

They already have—despite charging prices that are often the highest in the world. If it weren't for Indian dealers who have been cutting iolite in bulk and underpricing just about everyone else, iolite might be far more expensive than it is. Nevertheless, we expect the Germans to stick to their guns on prices, a reflection of their domination of the market and their confidence in iolite as an up-and-comer gem that will become to sapphire what NutraSweet has become to sugar.

BURMA JADEITE

Although jade is primarily associated with the Chinese, who have venerated it for more than 5,000 years, the gem owes its name to a group of far less well-known jade worshippers, the Mayans of Central America.

When the Spaniards conquered Central America in the early 16th century, they found many Mayans wearing the stone to ward off or cure kidney problems. This talismanic use inspired the Spaniards to call the gem: *piedra de l'ejade,* "stone of the loins." The French shortened it, with characteristic panache, to *le jade.*

Today Occidentals laugh at the superstition enshrined in the gem's name. But Orientals still take such beliefs seriously.

Yet even the East is bowing to modern jade custom.

The jade they wear for well-being is no longer the nephrite variety (a silicate of calcium and magnesium) that the Chinese revered and on which jade's reputation is largely based. Instead, they wear a Burmese jadeite (a silicate of sodium and aluminum)—to traditionalists an interloper jade of no consequence in the gem's long illustrious history. This jadeite was first imported into China late in the 18th century. Ironically, the jade the Spaniards first saw in the New World 150 or so years before was a cousin of Burmese jadeite found in Guatemala and possibly Costa Rica.

So, without knowing it, the conquistadors predicted our own time's preference for jadeite over nephrite when they coined the name the entire species is known by throughout the world.

But while its name is relatively new, basic attitudes about jade are ancient. In fact, the gem may be the only one that is still used as much for an amulet as for adornment. Experts estimate that millions of Orientals, Chinese especially, wear jadeite jewelry for good luck and health. "Within every Oriental there lurks a jade lover," says one Los Angeles jadeite specialist. It's easy to see why.

A CULTURAL MAINSTAY

For centuries, Chinese poets linked jade's attributes—the most famous: steel-like toughness—to those of the gods, while philosophers praised its virtues. So esteemed was China's native jade, the nephrite variety, that its emperors, accorded divine rights, spoke their prayers through ceremonial jade discs.

So why did Burmese jadeite quickly rob Chinese nephrite of regard? Because the most prized nephrite—a white, diaphanous variety called "mutton fat jade"—became too scarce, leaving carvers to work with the more common waxy green kind found today.

BURMA JADEITE

The green of this nephrite was no match for the lighter green of the jadeite first imported into China from neighboring Burma in 1784, after the two countries signed a trade pact. It was called *te t'sui*, which means "kingfisher feather," because its intense spectral green conjured up the color intensity of that bird's feathers (which, in actuality, are blue). Such color, coupled with the stone's luster and translucence, captivated Chinese carvers and artisans. Ever since, jadeite has been the jade of preference worldwide. Indeed, nephrite is valued mainly for its antiquity while jadeite is valued in and of itself.

A case in point: In 1965, a New York gem dealer bought an antique jadeite Chinese archer's ring for $735. After he had it cut into four cabochons, he got $10,000 for the stones.

That anecdote gives some idea of the tremendous value placed on fine jadeite. As a result, Chinese dealers will gamble tens, even hundreds, of thousands of dollars on jadeite rough (called "boulders")—weighing anywhere from a few kilos to hundreds of pounds—that they think will yield superb stones. The Chinese, for whom high-stakes gambling is second nature, will occasionally buy a rough based only on its outward appearance. "Surface flecks or stripes of green may embolden them to bid on a boulder," says one Miami jadeite importer.

More often, he continues, the Chinese will buy based on evaluation of the rough after a small window has been polished on its surface. "That gives more of an indication of the quality one can expect," he says, "but the risks are still enormous."

Although Burma is the sole source of fine jadeite and Thailand its prime entry point (via smugglers) into the jewelry world, Hong Kong is the gem-world capital for jadeite—indeed, all jade—today.

According to one jadeite specialist, Hong Kong dealers have very definite priorities when cutting jade rough. If a piece is free of streaks and fractures, and deep enough, it is earmarked for cutting into cabochons—easily the most desirable form of jadeite. Next come, in descending order, bangles, beads, carvings and discs (also known as "doughnuts"). Jadeite is most often cut into carvings, including, quite often, Buddhas, animals and crosses. Since jadeite is still used as a talisman, these carvings prove extremely popular, especially in pendant form.

QUALITY IN JADEITE

Jadeite comes in many colors (including lavender and red), but green is the color that is most coveted. Experts describe the ideal for this color in varying ways. One likens the finest green in jadeite to that of

BURMA JADEITE

liquid Prell concentrate shampoo. Another compares the color to "the intense green shoots of a freshly seeded lawn." Both are talking about what is called "imperial green," a color very often likened to that of the finest emerald. Stones that exhibit forest or spinach green are considered too dark; stones paler than a pleasing apple-green are too light.

But quality in jadeite isn't merely a matter of hue and tone. It is a function of several factors:

■ COLOR UNIFORMITY: Stones should be free of blotchiness that imparts an unevenness to the color.

■ TRANSLUCENCY: Stones should be semi-transparent in natural light.

■ CLARITY: Stones should be as inclusion-free as possible when illuminated from beneath by a fiber-optics or pen-light source.

■ BRIGHTNESS: Stones should exhibit a lustrous brilliance that some dealers describe as a glow.

When all these factors—hue, color uniformity, translucency, clarity and brightness—are present to a high degree, prices for 5-carat jadeite cabs will reach tens of thousands of dollars in the few fine jewelry stores that carry them. Larger top-caliber stones between 10 and 20 carats could cost $100,000, or even more.

But don't despair. Decent jadeites around 3 to 5 carats are available for a fraction of such prices. Of course, expect such stones to be nearly opaque to nearly translucent, veer to either light or dark tones, be somewhat included and lack the high polish of better jadeite. For a couple thousand dollars, however, consumers should be able to find nice apple-green stones with good translucency, clarity and brightness.

One warning when buying jadeite: A lot of it is dyed. So make sure your jeweler guarantees in writing that your jadeite has not been so enhanced.

KUNZITE

Kunzite is a much bad-mouthed beauty. At its best a deep-pink lavender, this spodumene is hard to set and, once set, inclined to fade. Nonetheless, kunzite deserves a place in the sun.

No, make that shade. Hot lights can, and do, turn this stone a whiter shade of pale, although color loss is usually very gradual. However, worn with an understanding of its high-strung traits, top kunzite can give enduring beauty equal to that of Ceylonese pink sapphire and Brazilian pink topaz—for vastly less money.

Unfortunately, the deep-pink/lavender varieties of spodumene are rarely seen in this country. More appreciative markets—Japan, in particular—are willing to pay higher prices for these scarce stones. So, instead, America sees weaker commercial colors whose pale strains of pink are hardly comparable in strength to those of fancy corundum. But it is not these wash-outs that we are talking about here, nor even next-step-up stones with a pleasing blush of lilac.

No, what we have in mind are kunzites with the electric-lavender color shown on the opposite page. This hue is rarely encountered in stones under 10 carats and can be the object of somewhat intensive searching in sizes below 15 carats. (The stone shown here weighs 38.8 carats.) Once you get to sizes above 20 carats, the search for deep colors eases considerably. At 30 carats, fine color is more common, but certainly not commonplace.

The trouble is that few jewelry store customers are in the market for 30-carat stones, even ones as relatively inexpensive from a per-carat price perspective as kunzite. Matters aren't helped much when shoppers hear that this spodumene—discovered in California early in this century and named after the pioneering gemologist and Tiffany's vice president George Frederick Kunz (1856-1932)—has a reputation for brittleness and color instability.

However, a growing number of jewelers think these negatives are overemphasized. "Kunzite is like opal," says a Wyoming kunzite specialist. "You've got to handle it with care. But that doesn't stop people from wearing and enjoying it."

AVOIDING THE CLEAVAGES

The Wyoming dealer, who has cut at least 5,000 carats of kunzite since 1970, believes the stone is a victim of "bum raps." Its reputation for brittleness, he says, comes from the fact that spodumene, very much like diamond, is plagued with cleavages (planes of crystal weakness). If cut improperly, these cleavages simply give way. "You just can't pick up a

KUNZITE

kunzite and start grinding it," the Wyoming dealer explains. "But the same can be said of tanzanite, a stone which can cleave even more easily." The need for extreme care also extends to setting polished stones.

"Heat is a no-no," he continues. "That means you must use a burnishing tool, not a torch, when setting. Further, you can't force the prongs or cracking could result. But once mounted—preferably in malleable 18k-gold prongs or perhaps a bezel setting—the stone is fairly durable."

While on the subject of heat, it is important to note that close proximity to high heat (whether from flame or lamp), as well as the ultraviolet rays of sunlight, will bleach out color, sometimes in moments, but most often over years. But these conditions, kunzite partisans quickly add, can also take a similar toll on pink topaz.

Although kunzite is a stone which shuns heat, it can't seem to escape it. Today, in fact, at least 50% of all kunzite sold has been subjected to either heating or irradiation, during which stones that started life light-grayish or bluish pinks turn cherry-blossom lavenders and light-plum purples.

It is very hard to tell treated from natural kunzite. But the Wyoming dealer thinks he has found a simple visual test to detect many treated stones. According to him, treating often destroys the trichroism—the display of different colors from different angles—that is the hallmark of kunzite. Consequently, stones take on a sameness of color, no matter from what direction they are viewed. Natural stones, on the other hand, will appear different colors when viewed in different directions. For instance, a stone that is lavender when seen through the table may appear slightly greenish when seen through the girdle.

THE AFGHAN CONNECTION

Because kunzite is a trichroic stone, it is critical to orient the stone properly when first cut. That means cutting along its C-axis for optimum color (which ranges from lavender pink to lavender bluish-pink). Generally, this is what is done.

All too frequently, however, stones are cut with big windows that rob them, in the Wyoming dealer's words, of "full fire and color intensity." When perfectly cut, he continues, fine-color stones "are the equal of medium-pink sapphire. And being an extremely transparent material to begin with, kunzite has far more life than, say, pink tourmaline whose colors are usually darker and brilliance therefore more masked."

Deep-lavender kunzite, while a relative rarity, is a bit more common now that Afghanistan has replaced Brazil as the gem's main source. It

KUNZITE

did so by default. According to one Manhattan-based Brazilian gem expert, Brazil hasn't produced material in at least 25 years. "Whatever stones you see from Brazil are old goods that have been hoarded for decades," he says, "or new material from Afghanistan."

Although Afghanistan has been actively mining kunzite since about 1978, production there hit its greatest stride in 1984-85. Then the country's main producing area in Nooristan, a stronghold of rebel resistance against the Soviet invasion of 1979, came under constant bombardment and mining plunged to about 20% of what it had been. Now that the Soviet Union has withdrawn its troops, it is hoped that production will quickly reach, maybe even surpass, former peaks, especially since the reputation of Afghanistan's kunzites has overshadowed the Brazilian variety.

That fame couldn't come at a better time. Pastel-pink gems are currently enjoying enormous fashion popularity and kunzite is one of the pink gems to have benefited most from the vogue.

Besides its color, the fact that kunzite, unlike, say, rubellite, is generally clean (important to pastel-color stones) has helped boost this gem's reputation. Kunzite would probably enjoy even greater usage if stones with better color were more often bite- rather than boulder-sized. Roughs are so very large that they frequently yield 50-carat polished stones. Indeed, one New York gem dealer has a pet 170-carat Afghan stone of deep-pink color that he takes to gem shows as a showpiece—and as living proof that the species can stand up to more heat than it is generally given credit for. "I've kept that kunzite under hot display lights for 100 days running with no sign of fading," he says.

"Even so," the New Yorker quickly adds, "it's probably best to consider kunzite an evening stone." That's pretty much the consensus about this species. As the Wyoming dealer advises: "Kunzite is not for the beach or the golf course. But if you're in a place like Miami and you want to wear it in daylight, just try to stay off the sunny side of the street."

LAPIS LAZULI

During the spring of 1985, lapis lazuli, of all things, became a hot topic on Capitol Hill.

The subject first came up during Senate Armed Services Committee hearings on Afghanistan, the prime source of lapis and the scene of a then six-year-old war between Moslem rebels and the Soviet-backed government of Babrak Karmal. Moslem freedom fighters testified that sales of lapis rough were a major means by which they raised cash for arms needed to fight invading Russian troops.

Ironically, the rebels may well have borrowed the idea of selling lapis to raise weapons money from their opponents. In early 1984, the government of Afghanistan advertised an auction for tons of lapis rough.

Of all the many gems found in Afghanistan (the country also produces ruby, emerald and kunzite, among other species), lapis most readily lends itself to being used as a cash cow for weapons procurement. As a lapis source, Afghanistan has no competition in terms of quantity or quality. While the Soviet Union mines this mineral on a limited basis, the only other sizeable supply is found in Chile whose softer, paler, slightly greenish material has no following among connoisseurs or dealers.

That left war-torn Afghanistan with a de facto monopoly on this venerable blue beauty. Still, the idea of buying lapis to help finance a war was a bit jarring since the gem has long been associated with peace—at least spiritual peace. At one point, the ancients mistakenly called lapis "sapphirus" because of its deep heavenly blue. But even after this confusion was corrected, the gem preserved its connection with the firmament when it was given the name it is still known by, lapis lazuli—a mixture of Latin (*lapis* for stone) and Arabic (*allazward* for sky blue) meaning literally "azure stone."

Given such connotations, it is hardly surprising that the Sumerians—the supreme lapis lovers of antiquity—were willing to spend years traveling from one end of Asia to the other on mining expeditions for the gem. Author Benjamin Zucker relates in his book "A Connoisseur's Guide to Gems and Jewelry" that during the Middle Ages ruling class art patrons demanded that painters use blue made from ground lapis, by then known as "ultramarine." Men of less means had to tolerate cheaper, second-string blue pigments made from indigo or copper.

Today, interest in lapis is as strong as it has ever been—only now it's decidedly secular. Nevertheless, the lapis market looks to grow even stronger now that the stone with heaven's blue has become a men's ring mainstay. Prospects are good, in fact, that it will gain even more ground with males—especially if supplies remain what they've been.

LAPIS LAZULI

BOULDERS OF BLUE

There are literally tons of lapis for sale these days. According to a major importer of lapis rough based in San Francisco, the European, Asian and American markets are glutted with material. As with most gems, the majority of the material is only so-so. Out of, say, five tons, the importer estimates that only 1,015 kilos will be decent and as little as two kilos "top quality."

By top quality, most dealers mean stones with a deep uniform blue (often tinged with violet) that are free of white calcite veining the surface and virtually free of more tolerable golden pyrite flecks. Some lapis lovers, however, like their stones to show pyrite, but they are a minority among connoisseurs. One other noteworthy plus: The very best lapis should have a high polish. Since stones vary in hardness, one can encounter fine color and poor polish (evidence of a softer stone).

One notch below fine comes what one New York lapis expert calls "B-grade" lapis. Such stones may be dyed in spots, but never in their entirely, to conceal small patches of calcite. Most of the time, however, they are all-natural with either lighter shades of even blue, slight to mild color zoning of darker blues, or, perhaps, some surface cracks.

Last is dyed lapis. Despite waxing to seal in color additives, dyes used in lapis are unstable, especially if exposed to household chemicals such as lighter fluid. Perspiration, perfumes and cosmetics also pose a constant threat to dyed lapis beads and forced many a jeweler to put up with returns of dyed lapis necklaces.

Therefore, it is important to ask retailers if the lapis jewelry pieces they offer are dyed, a virtual certainty when buying lapis beads. But even where beads aren't involved, price can be a giveaway. A 16-inch strand of dyed 8mm beads, a very popular item, will cost one-half to one-quarter an undyed one.

But don't always depend on price to tip you off to dyeing. Some retailers who paid their suppliers a higher price for what they were assured is natural lapis may be unwittingly passing on their mistakes to customers. So you might ask them to spot check stones in your presence by dabbing them with cotton swabs dipped in acetone. Sometimes even licking suspect lapis with the tongue and then wiping the stone on a piece of tissue paper will leave a tell-tale blue streak. In any case, have the merchant put in writing that the stones are natural and undyed.

LAPIS LAZULI

A FAVORITE WITH MEN

Lapis is one of the world's most popular men's gems, second perhaps only to black onyx. Although far more expensive in top grades than black onyx, lapis is still inexpensive in comparison to prices fetched for it seven to eight years ago.

But all that may change if and when disclosure of treatment becomes more of an industry norm. Candor at the jewelry counter will eventually squeeze prices for limited-supply undyed goods sharply higher.

Given the enormous prevalence of dyed lapis in today's market, it seems incredible how many jewelry manufacturers insist that they do not use treated material. When pressed, some we talked to qualified their assurances to hold only for rings. They were far more evasive about stones used for earrings. "Quality isn't generally as important in an earring as it is a ring," one New Jersey manufacturer told us.

When buying lapis, consumers should not only be on the lookout for dyed material but also synthetic stones that are laboratory duplications of nature. Even more pesky to lapis buyers are blue calcite-veined sodalites (properly, but hardly ever, called hackmanites) from places like America, Canada, Greenland and Norway. Costing next to nothing, these lapis look-alikes can fool the unwary. And no wonder. Both stones belong to the same rock family, sodium aluminum silicate. To make matters worse, sodalite laps up dye as readily as most of its more expensive next of kin. (Fortunately, sodalite gives itself away by its lower specific gravity—2.24, on average, versus 2.75, on average—and can be easily tested by your jeweler).

But don't be scared. For the most part, consumers are more likely to see lapis from Afghanistan than sodalite from America. "There's as much lapis as people want," one importer says, "provided they want commercial grades."

MOONSTONE

Consumers who plan to purchase fine blue moonstones might have to delay their plans indefinitely now that the world's main vein for this gem in Sri Lanka has run bone dry. What remains in the way of this orthoclase member of the many-branched feldspar family are mostly run-of-the-mill stones that resemble water with milk of magnesia stirred in. For an idea of what used to be, feast your eyes on the photo that we've used to illustrate this species. Alas, it shows what is probably a nearly, if not already, extinct variety of this gem that many Europeans, principally Germans, often found lovely enough to encircle with diamonds.

As luck would have it, U.S. jewelers just began to learn of this kind of moonstone when practically none could be found. Why few retailers in the States ever knew such moonstones existed is a mystery. But those few in the know call them "blue-sheen" stones, the name they go by in Europe. At their best, they are invariably crystal clear with a floating blue to blue-white opalescence on their surface.

A decade ago, when larger blue-sheen moonstones were very plentiful, consumers could buy them for prices comparable to those of the cheapest semiprecious stones. Nowadays prices for such stones can easily be five to 10 times what they were back then. But what can jewelers do? The sole source for blue sheens, Meetiyagoda in Sri Lanka, ceased production in 1987. "All most dealers have left are tiny little stones, nothing of any consequence," says a buyer for a New York cabochon and bead stone importing company. "So it looks like those who want the blue-sheen material in decent sizes are going to have to depend on antique and estate pieces from now on."

INSTEAD OF PEARLS

The bleak news about blue-sheen moonstone puts jewelers who sell this gem in a bit of a quandary. A birthstone for June, moonstone is usually considered an alternate to pearl—at least in America. In Europe, where some birthstone lists actually place moonstone ahead of pearl, it is often the other way around: Pearl is a substitute for moonstone. And for very good reason: national pride.

One of the earliest and best sources of moonstone was St. Gotthard in Switzerland, formerly known as Mount Adular, from which is derived the root of moonstone's old name, adularia. Although that name is rarely used today, gemologists around the world refer to moonstone's sheen as "adularescence," which means that it results from the interplay of light with layers of tiny albite crystals in these stones. The thinner the layer, the bluer the sheen; the thicker, the whiter. Strictly speaking, the term

MOONSTONE

adularescence is just a synonym for the more widely known term "opalescence." But don't tell that to moonstone aficionados—not those in German-speaking countries. Pride in the gem's once local origins, plus its mainstay status, keep them calling the sheen phenomenon by the name of adularescence.

When choosing moonstones, European connoisseurs look for two things: ideal body and sheen color. What's the ideal? For body color, it's completely colorless transparency; for sheen, it's a deep, haunting sky blue which glides across the dome or table of a stone as it is moved against the light.

Like most ideals, the one for moonstone is rarely attained. A Los Angeles-based moonstone expert estimates that, at most, one out of every 100 Sri Lankan moonstones ever qualified as "blue." What are known as "semi-blue" and "silver-white" stones were sometimes passed off as blue sheen, but they didn't rank as true-blue moonstones.

Years ago, when Burma was a big producer of blue-sheen goods, there was no need to stretch this term so far out of bounds. But, based on reports from dealers who travel regularly to Thailand, where most new Burma gem production is smuggled to market, Burma—like Sri Lanka—can no longer be counted on for any more than an intermittent handful of blue beauties. Although America, Mexico and Tanzania, among others, produce moonstone also, output is sparse and far from the ideal.

This leaves jewelers who wish to stick with moonstone little choice but to make do with lesser grades. Don't get us wrong. Some of the skim-milk blues to sage-beard whites are very lovely. Moreover, with their soft, lustrous appearance, it is easy to understand why birthstone list compilers assigned moonstone an understudy role for pearl. Its low cost is certainly a consoling factor. What's more, prices drop very sharply for stones whose body color becomes increasingly brownish or which show the tiny stress marks that are a characteristic of this stone. Or one can desert blue sheen entirely in favor of special effect moonstones and even other feldspars altogether.

STARS, EYES AND RAINBOWS

Many highly cloudy moonstones, some with strong body color, are cut into high-domed cabochons so that their sheen collects in a chatoyant silver-white band across the top. These stones are known as "cat's-eye moonstones" and are readily available in 10- to 20-carat sizes. Occasionally, cat's-eye moonstones have a second band, or ray, intersecting the first at a right angle. Some dealers call these stones with cross-

MOONSTONE

shaped eyes "star moonstones."

Retailers who seek stones more nearly reminiscent of conventional moonstone may be interested in a new-variety feldspar, properly called bytownite, coming out of India. These stones are called "rainbow moonstones" because they feature a multicolored adularescence. The finest have a reddish-orange or sometimes a lavender sheen with areas of green and blue. Lesser grades have a more predominantly brownish sheen.

After only a few years on the market, the very finest rainbow moonstones in scarce 10-carat sizes already command as much as fine blue-sheen moonstones—an amazing feat when you consider that this gem is a virtual unknown. A southern California moonstone specialist says fierce German buying of this gem at often heady prices has crowded out more fainthearted American buyers unable to accept prices for a new-entry feldspar that have outdistanced those for blue-sheen moonstone in no time at all.

Rather than face high prices, however, some American dealers blame their difficulties finding the new rainbow moonstone on supply when, in reality, the situation stems more from demand. Goods are bypassing the U.S. market because of voracious foreign consumption at what are untenable prices in the U.S. importer market.

Meanwhile, a few last pointers when buying moonstone, conventional or otherwise. Those new to this gem should bear in mind that moonstones have a far-from-rugged hardness of 6-6½ on the Mohs scale. Often they also have strong cleavages. The bottom line: Wear these gems with care, especially if they are mounted in rings.

MORGANITE

Naming new-found gem and mineral species after those who discovered them or in honor of important mineralogists and gemologists has been accepted practice for at least a century. But in 1911, the mineral world made a notable exception to this custom for a pink beryl that had recently been discovered on the African island of Madagascar.

At the urging of gemology and jewelry kingpin George Kunz, the new stone was called "morganite," ostensibly to honor banker/financier John Pierpont Morgan for his many donations of gems and minerals to the American Museum of Natural History. Among Morgan's gifts to the museum: the much-celebrated 16,000-piece Clarence Bementh mineral collection bought in 1900 for the then princely sum of $100,000.

But, in actuality, paying tribute to Morgan for his munificence was a secondary reason for the name choice. Kunz was far more likely paying an IOU to Morgan incurred for a failure to honor his generosity eight years earlier.

At the time, J.P. Morgan was perhaps the most distinguished patron of Tiffany's, the much-heralded jewelry store for which Kunz worked as a vice president. Kunz had often arranged for Morgan to buy collections direct from Tiffany, or with the store acting as intermediary, that the tycoon would then donate.

To show his appreciation, Kunz, according to a 1922 article that he wrote, proposed that a new-found species of pink spodumene, discovered in California in 1902, be named "morganite." But when Morgan supposedly couldn't be reached to OK the intended trade name, Charles Baskerville, a chemistry professor with whom Kunz collaborated on the first gemological studies of the new gem, suggested, instead, the name "kunzite."

Kunz expert Lawrence Conklin doubts the gemologist made any real effort to reach Morgan or that much persuasion was needed to get him to accept the 1903 name substitution. "Kunz was a very clever man and something of a promoter," Conklin says. "I think he wanted that spodumene named after himself in the worst way." If so, did a lingering guilty conscience years later prompt Kunz to christen the next pink gem he was instrumental in identifying "morganite"?

We'll probably never know the answer to this question. In any case, the beryl's trade name is a reminder of Kunz's power in the gem world during the late 19th and early 20th centuries. What's more, it is fitting that the trade names of two often-confused pink gems—kunzite and morganite—should bear witness to Tiffany's turn-of-the-century hegemony in colored stones, one for which Kunz was primarily responsible.

MORGANITE

THE DEEPEST OF PINKS

By 1911, when the new pink beryl entered the marketplace, Tiffany had already scored marketing triumphs with the pink shades of two other gem species: tourmaline and spodumene. Now it could give the public a triumvirate of choices in this color.

Those first African morganites were indeed spectacular, sporting, in the words of beryl authorities John Sinkankis and Peter G. Read, writing in their 1986 book "Beryl," "a unique magenta tint that suggests the color of high-quality kunzite." Given the gem's namesake, it is fitting that some of the most prized specimens of cut morganite from Madagascar can be found in the museum that owes so much to J.P. Morgan, the American Museum of Natural History.

Unfortunately, Madagascar is no longer an active producer of morganite. Today the world has to make do with paler rose-pink beryls, mostly from Brazil. To get some idea of the general color strength of modern-day morganites, imagine lighter tones of morganite's very common blue sister species, aquamarine. At their best, these stones exhibit a very sweet blush pink that could not be confused, as older stones from Madagascar might be, with the deep lilac hues of the top-grade kunzites currently coming from Afghanistan. As a result, says a Brazilian stone specialist, "you'll need 15- to 20-carat sizes for good body color. The color in smaller stones tends to wash out against the skin."

Finding decent-color morganites in larger sizes isn't easy. Maybe that is why the stone makes its sole stir these days in collector circles where stones that are somewhat pale in color are tolerated because people know the pickings are slim. To compensate for faint color, morganite collectors often insist that stones are at least brilliant—the byproduct of fine cutting. "Stones that are well cut," says one dealer, "have a wonderful glow in subdued light."

FROM PEACH TO PINK

When Brazilian morganites are first mined, many have a peach-orange color that is often so attractive that it has generated its own market. In fact, many connoisseurs will tell you that no morganite collection is complete without a first-rate example of peach color.

But watch out. If such stones are subjected to prolonged sunlight through everyday wearing or even being left on a window sill for as little as a week, they will turn a permanent pastel pink. That's why many of the morganites one sees today are products of the heat-treater's art. They started life a peach color but were then put in an oven to turn them

MORGANITE

pink. "Those who want their peach morganites to stay peach had better consider them as evening stones," the Brazilian gem specialist warns.

That morganite must be kept indoors to keep it from turning pink is a bit ironic when you remember that this gem's nearest rival, kunzite, must be kept pretty much indoors to keep it from losing its pink. This fact may be the seed of a wonderful selling point in morganite's favor. "One of kunzite's greatest drawbacks is its color instability," a dealer says. "Morganite's pink is more stable."

And while we're on the subject of morganite's advantages vis-à-vis kunzite, we might as well remind readers that kunzite is plagued by cleavage problems. This makes it a much riskier ring stone than morganite.

Nevertheless, we don't want to build up morganite at kunzite's expense, especially since today's mainstay pink (as opposed to peach) morganite rarely rivals today's mainstay kunzite for color saturation. And even if it did, there would still be no contest between the two in terms of production. Although far from abundant, kunzite is blessed with its greatest availability in years. Morganite, on the other hand, is so scarce it remains mostly a curiosity. The San Diego dealer notes there was a gap of 15 years before miners in Brazil recently hit a pocket of truly worthwhile morganite. "And that material was gone in almost no time at all," he says.

AUSTRALIAN BLACK OPAL

O, the power of the pen. With just one strange plot twist in his 1829 bestseller, "Anne of Geierstein," Sir Walter Scott destroyed the European opal market for nearly 50 years. And he did it just by having a character falsely accused of being a demoness die shortly after a chance drop of holy water fell on her opal and quenched its mysterious, fiery color. Convinced Scott was warning them that wearing opal could bring bad luck, suggestible readers stopped buying the gem. Within a matter of months, the opal market had crashed and prices were down more than 50%.

It took a remarkable find of black opal at Lightning Ridge in New South Wales, Australia, in 1877, to revive the market for this gem. Australia's spectacular new opals took the world by storm. Indeed, there have been almost no opals found in the last 50 years to match what came from Lightning Ridge in its late 19th and early 20th century heyday. No wonder dealers sometimes liken Lightning Ridge's impact and significance to that of Kashmir for sapphire, a Himalayan source discovered around the same time, that set the standard for sapphire in the same way Lightning Ridge did for opal.

To get some idea of the aesthetic standard set by Lightning Ridge material, pause now and study the picture on the facing page. The gem you see there is a magnificent example of Lightning Ridge opal, one that came from a dealer's private collection and is assumed to be turn-of-the-century. Nothing like it has been known to come from Australia in decades. So rare is this stone that it almost seems sadistic to use it to illustrate the ideal for black opal beauty. On the other hand, when dealers describe perfection for this gem, they invariably have such stones in mind—exceptional though they are.

Not that stones like it can't be found. But they won't be found any longer on the opal fields of Australia. A few might come up for sale at auction or be bought from estates by the more elite jewelry salons of America or Europe. Still, the best chance of finding classic black opal lies in Japan, whose people are so fond of this gem that the market is almost theirs alone.

According to one Maryland opal wholesaler, Japan consumes at least 50%, and perhaps as much as 70%, of the world's black opal production. "Knowing that fine black opal can bring huge sums in Japan, Australian dealers pay more for stones on the opal fields than they could ever hope to sell them for here in the United States," he says.

Because the Japanese are willing to pay so much, especially for 2- to 4-carat stones, U.S. opal specialists devote less than 10% of their inventories to black opal. Instead, they concentrate on white opal. "America

AUSTRALIAN BLACK OPAL

is to white opal what Japan is to black," says a one New York opal dealer. Why is black opal so much less popular here?

LIGHTNING STRIKES ONCE

Black opal is far rarer than white opal. In fact, there are only two active black opal localities in the world, both in Australia. Of the two, the older, Lightning Ridge, is said to be the only one to produce true black opal. The other, Mintabe, is known more for gray-to-grayish-black material. Some purists even protest calling Mintabe stones black opal. They do so on both geological and aesthetic grounds.

Traditionally, black opal was considered a variety of opal found in rock formations called nodules (or "nobbies" in the trade) as opposed to white opal which is found in seams. But when Mintabe, whose opal is also found in seams, was discovered, this geology-based distinction began to blur—at least among dealers.

One can see why opal dealers insist that Mintabe's dark-gray material be accorded full standing as black opal. If they had to restrict their definition to goods from fast-depleting Lightning Ridge, the future of this gem would be in grave doubt. For even when production from Lightning Ridge and Mintabe are pooled together, there is still far less black than white opal. Given its relative scarcity, black opal has never lent itself to volume jewelry use the way white opal has. As a result, black opal remains primarily a special order stone in this country. But the few who buy it here generally look for the same things the Japanese do: base color, hue mixture and color pattern.

BASICS OF OPAL BEAUTY

When dealers evaluate black opal, they start with its base color. The darker the base—or what dealers call "potch"—of an opal, the more pronounced and vivid its color. That's because an opal's beauty is the product of the contrast between its color play and its background.

As for ideal color in black opal, most experts look for the predominance of red and then orange. "Stones that appear all or almost all red are the most coveted," one dealer explains. "Increasing amounts of blue and green will reduce their value."

But specific color isn't all that connoisseurs want in a fine black opal. The pattern that they take is equally important. For years, the most prized pattern was what dealers call the "harlequin": well-defined squares, rectangles, triangles or diamonds of color in both symmetrical and asymmetrical designs.

AUSTRALIAN BLACK OPAL

Today, unfortunately, the harlequin pattern is encountered only in older pieces. No new stones with this pattern have been mined in years.

Failing to find stones with big blocks or even chunks of color, connoisseurs must content themselves instead with swirls. Often you'll hear them describe the best patterns that can be hoped for in black opal today as stones that exhibit broad well-defined flashes of color (called "rolling flash" in the trade) that change kaleidoscopically as stones are turned in the hand. Yet even these patterns are far from plentiful.

Realistically, the top black opals that consumers are likely to be offered nowadays feature color patterns comprised, at their best, of lively pointillistic dots. As these dots get smaller and less vivid, they come to resemble what the trade calls "pin fire." Such black opals are the most commonly found and least expensive.

FEARS OF CRACKING

Because opal is gelled silica, containing as much as 20% water, some of it tends to dry out and crack after being mined. This can happen almost immediately upon being taken from the ground or years later. The phenomenon is called "crazing" and it wipes out the value of a stone.

However, it is often supposed that black opal has a lower water content than white and that therefore it is more stable. But no one knows for sure.

To prevent crazing, some dealers recommend sealing stones with oil or leaving them in jars of water. Gemologists aren't sure if these measures will help.

That leaves consumers one last line of defense. Ask your jeweler if he bought the stone you're considering from a supplier who lived with his opal for some time before he sold it. If he did, chances are good that he'll have weeded out most of the bad stones.

AUSTRALIAN WHITE OPAL

Real estate wasn't the only casualty of the 1981 news that the rule of Hong Kong would be transferred from capitalist Britain to Communist China in 1997. The island's thriving white opal market was trampled in the same panic that killed its 10-year building boom.

For more than a decade, Hong Kong had been the undisputed center for white opal, responsible for cutting at least 90% of the world's supply. Like most of the colony's successful businessmen, Hong Kong's opal czars had fortunes tied up in local real estate and stock market speculation. News of the change in rulership burst both bubbles. "There were lots of bankruptcies in 1982," says a Maryland-based opal importer. "Dealers had no capital, so they couldn't finance old inventories or afford to build new ones."

By 1985, estimates a New York opal specialist, the number of cutting firms in Hong Kong had shriveled to fewer than 30 from more than 100 a decade earlier.

Even so, the world opal market remained remarkably composed. Australia, whose Coober Pedy and Andamooka mines account for at least 75% of the world's annual white opal supply, responded to the crisis by cutting back mining to about 40% of pre-crash levels. That kept the glut of opal temporarily in check. What's more, American, European and Japanese dealers quickly moved in to mop up any excess.

In the end, Hong Kong's opal woes were purely domestic, having far more to do with fear than fashion. Most, if not all, of the island's opal dealers and cutters are Chinese refugees or their children who left the mainland after Mao Tse-tung's takeover in 1949. Many spared the worst of the 1982 crash still chose to sell out lock, stock and barrel and move to places like America, Canada and Australia. In fact, the Maryland importer bought out three opal firms himself.

Ironically, the melt-down of Hong Kong's opal market has been followed by a modest heat up of opal sales—after years in the doldrums. Be advised, however, that "doldrums" in the opal market means something entirely different than it does in, say, the diamond market.

PRETTY FOR PENNIES

Throughout the 1980s, inexpensive karat-gold colored stone earrings have become more and more of a fashion mainstay. Mass merchandisers have found opal an ideal choice for such earrings. For extremely little money, white opal provides one of the cheapest and most abundant colored stone options, especially for finished karat-gold goods in the $20-$40 retail price range. Indeed, an important Providence, R.I. maker

AUSTRALIAN WHITE OPAL

of such earrings tells us his already robust opal business doubled in one year recently, then jumped another 20% the following year. "I'd have to say opal is coming back," he declares.

Actually, it never really went away. From a volume standpoint, opal has always been a major mover. Even in its off years in the late 1970s and early 1980s, white opal was a costume jewelry staple. But no one noticed because all the volume translated, one opal dealer estimates, into less than $50 million here, $100 million worldwide. Much of what sold in the off years was essentially low-end material. According to the New York dealer, this opal takes two basic forms: 1) milky white with pale multi-colored pinfire, or 2) blue green to green with broad flashes of color.

Because a large amount of low-end opal is used in earrings, easier-to-match pinfire is used more often than broad flash. At present, calibrated fancy shapes (ovals and pears) in 6x4mm to 8x6mm sizes (25-80 points) hold sway, a departure from the past. Until very recently, rounds (between 2-4mm) were the hottest shape. "Now they're dead," complains the Providence earring maker.

UP THE LADDER

Consumers who pride themselves on wearing quality will probably not be happy with largely opaque, pale, no-color-play opal—no matter how cheap. This opal hardly lives up to its name, derived, in part, from the Greek word *opallios* which means "to see a color change." But to get stones with an interesting array of color, plus some translucency, expect to pay a lot more than is asked for run-of-the-mill anemic opal. Stones that boast strong foreground reds, greens and blues are definitely not available at trinket prices.

The next step up is what dealers call "crystal opal." This term refers to the look and not the structure of stones. These opals sport, in one dealer's words, "a translucent glass-like appearance with full colors seemingly suspended in a transparent base."

But "crystal opal" is only one of the varieties of better opal. The finest usually show no identifiable background color—just a continuous, unbroken array of vivid color patches or patterns. These stones will cost about the same as better aquamarine or imperial topaz.

Although commercial-grade opal is largely what jewelry manufacturers use these days, there seem to be strong stirrings of interest in better goods. "Providence is definitely upgrading," the New York dealer states. Such upgrading means that manufacturers are overcoming past

AUSTRALIAN WHITE OPAL

resistance to opal based on what dealers say are exaggerated fears about durability.

IMPROVING THE ODDS

To be sure, many white opals crack, mainly through dehydration. But the problem can be minimized a lot more than jewelers think. It all has to do with dealer quality control.

First, the knowledgeable dealer knows which locations in Australia produce the most stable opal (Andamooka is famous for such stones), and shops accordingly. As an extra safeguard, some dealers hold all polished stones for several weeks and return any that crack.

Second, because those opals that crack tend to do so sooner rather than later, the responsible dealer will refrain from selling newly purchased or polished stones for a certain period of time to let nature weed out any losers. Dealers we interviewed call this procedure "curing" and subject both rough and cut stones to it.

Unfortunately, the dealer's ounce of prevention is often undone by the retailer's pound of abuse.

Since those opals with a high water content are the most prone to cracking (also called "crazing"), prolonged exposure to bright lights in a closed, unventilated showcase is an invitation to trouble. Thankfully, cracks are often skin deep and can be buffed out on a polisher's wheel.

MEXICAN FIRE OPAL

"Psst, want to buy an opal?"

It's not exactly what you'd expect to hear in the thronging tourist thoroughfares of Mexico City as one shops for native wares. But, believe it or not, this silicate is a common street corner commodity throughout the country's tourist areas. And it has been so for years. "I couldn't believe my eyes," says gemologist Cap Beesley about his first trip to Mexico City 21 years ago in search of opal. "Everyone was hustling the stuff."

Few Americans are ready for the sight of opal in profusion during their stays south of the border. That's understandable, since the gem is associated with Australia. Nevertheless, while no rival to Australia in terms of production, Mexico has come into its own as an opal source. Indeed, the country's opal is so distinctively different from Aussie material that it has earned its own name, fire opal, and its own following.

But don't expect to be shown connoisseur-class material on Mexico City's crowded sidewalks or even in its more private alleys—unless you're prepared to spend days looking. The country's street-corner opals are often similar in quality to the street-corner rubies so many GIs brought back home from Thailand during the Vietnam War.

Dealers who specialize in Mexican fire opal, of which there are probably fewer than half a dozen in America, find their chances of buying the more venerable varieties of this stone much better at American gem shows and far better yet in Idar-Oberstein where savvy German cutters have been importing most of Mexico's best opal rough for decades.

Occasionally, American dealers trek to Mexico's opal mines to bargain directly for the rough. But ever since the U.S. dollar went into free fall against the deutsche mark in 1985, bidding for rough has become a one-sided arm-wrestle in favor of the Germans. Worse, the dollar's decline has roughed up domestic trade in polished stones because now the Japanese—the world's most ardent admirers of black opal—have taken a strong yen to this gem. Unless the dollar's rout is significantly reversed, some U.S. dealers fear that fine Mexican fire opal could pretty much vanish from their inventories. That would be a pity.

GREAT BALLS OF FIRE

At their best, Mexican fire opals possess either flaming-orange or cherry-red body color that is uniform and solid—as opposed to the iridescent streaks, patches or flecks of color in fine Australian opal. That's why use of the term "fire" with this breed of opal is a bit incongruous since it usually refers to play of color not, as in the case of Mexican material, to body color. In any case, if roughs are transparent or sufficiently translu-

MEXICAN FIRE OPAL

cent, they will be faceted rather than cut into cabochons.

This isn't to say that Mexico doesn't produce Australian-like color-play opal suitable for cabochon cutting, the standard cut with opal. According to a West German cutter, top color-play opals from Mexico rival those from Down Under except that the Mexican variety—also known as "contra luz opal"—tend to array their colors against orange, instead of white, backgrounds. Since scarce better-to-fine Mexican color-play cabs in sizes over 2 carats currently command wholesome amounts in the Japanese market, U.S. jewelers understandably prefer far more abundant and reasonably priced Australian stones.

But when it comes to deep-body-color opals, whether cabbed or faceted, they have no choice. Mexican stones are the only game in town. At present, it's a game with relatively few stateside players. And if the dollar weakens significantly again, the number of players will only decrease. "With fire opal becoming more popular in strong-currency countries like Japan, cutters in Idar find they can ask significantly more for stones," explains a Connecticut-based fire opal specialist. "Consequently, the market is shifting more and more abroad because jewelers in this country aren't ready yet to absorb steady price jumps."

No doubt about it, prices for fine fire opal are climbing, easily 40% in the last few years, with most of the gains in the past year or so. Yet despite its surging cost, the stone still strikes us as affordable, especially in light of its scarcity.

THE CRAZING FACTOR

Like all opal, the Mexican variety can crack in the course of time. What percentage of stones will be so afflicted is impossible to say. One New York opal dealer is of the opinion that most Mexican stones are inherently unstable. But he's quick to admit that he lacks actual experience cutting or marketing this material.

Fire opal specialists do not deny that crazing is a problem. But they quickly add that the problem is exaggerated. Further, they believe that they effectively circumvent it by subjecting stones to fairly intensive screening.

"First of all, we put stones on a mild heat radiator set at 80 degrees Fahrenheit for 10 days," the West German cutter says. "If problems develop, the stone is rejected." If problems don't emerge, that doesn't mean the stone is out of the woods. The German cutter estimates that about 10% of the stones that make it past this initial heat test will start to crack up during the first stages of cutting, otherwise known as pre-

MEXICAN FIRE OPAL

forming. Tiny milky dots or larger spots are generally telltale signs that the stone could possibly go to pieces if kept on the wheel. Although some cutters immediately throw away such pieces, there are those who may not be so scrupulous. Beesley remembers being shown some partially formed street-corner opals in Mexico that were incompletely cut because cracking had developed while processing them. To disguise cracks, sellers had bathed stones in oil. This practice is hardly restricted to the tourist opals of Mexico.

As for stones which make it unscathed through cutting, there may be one or two which crack later. But specialists we talked to insist this almost never happens. "I've sold 1,500 stones in the last decade without one problem," the Connecticut dealer says. He attributes his good luck with fire opal to his fastidious selection process of rough material.

While not as fortunate as the New Englander with regard to crazing, the European, a major processor of fire opal, says screening has, for the most part, spared him from customer complaints. Even so, he takes no chances. "Since troubles occur within a short time after stones leave my inventory, I guarantee every fire opal I sell for one year from date of sale," he says.

Because fire opal, like all opal, is somewhat high-strung, it is best to consider it a fragile stone, far more appropriate for use in pendants or earrings than in rings. This is not to rule out ring use altogether. But jewelers who sell stones in such settings will feel an ethical obligation to advise customers about the consequences of lackadaisical, everyday wearing.

AMERICAN FRESHWATER PEARL

Sandwiched between the California gold rush of 1848 and the South African diamond rush of 1868 is a far less remembered but no less frenzied hunt for one of nature's treasures: the New Jersey pearl rush of 1857.

It all started in the spring of that year when a northern New Jersey shoemaker discovered a pearl weighing nearly 100 carats in a stream mussel he had caught and fried. If he had extracted the pearl before the heat of cooking destroyed its luster, it would have been worth, estimates famed turn-of-the-century gemologist George Kunz, $25,000—making it the most valuable pearl of the age.

News of the find sparked an instant flurry of stream and river mussel gathering. When, a few days later, a carpenter was paid $1,500 by Charles L. Tiffany for a second notable pearl, this one deep pink and weighing just under 25 carats, no stream or river in the upper part of New Jersey was safe from swarms of pearl hunters. Within less than five years, the area had been picked practically clean of unios, America's freshwater pearl-bearing mollusk, and the fever went into latency until its next outbreak in 1878, this time in southwestern Ohio. From there, it spread west and south, finally reaching its region of greatest intensity—the Mississippi River tributary system—in 1889.

If there was one area where the fever became a fury, it was the Mississippi system, whose Pecatonica River in Wisconsin gave mussel gatherers their first delirious taste of this country's greatest pearl riches. By 1891, when Wisconsin pearl recovery was in full swing, the state accounted for a record $300,000 worth of high-grade freshwater pearls. In 1900, it was joined in pearl grandeur by Tennessee and Arkansas, and in 1906 by Illinois.

Yet all the while U.S. pearl hunting was reaching new heights, gemologists were sounding warnings about its impact on the environment. "Many ponds and small river basins have been so denuded that not for many years, if ever, can they recover their former wealth of pearl-bearers," a worried Kunz wrote in his 1908 masterpiece, "The Book of the Pearl." But somehow pearl fishing was still a sizeable and unrestrained pursuit at the time of his death in 1932.

OF BUTTONS AND BEADS

The growth of American pearling was undoubtedly abetted by the development of a prosperous mother-of-pearl button industry late in the 19th century. For decades, until the introduction of imitations, those buttons were made from the iridescent linings of the millions of unio shells gathered annually in pearl fishing.

AMERICAN FRESHWATER PEARL

Today this mollusk's shell is still used in industry, principally, and somewhat ironically, to make the bead nucleii that forms the inside of the Japanese cultured pearl. What's more, divers still hunt for pearls in unios, hoping to sell them to the few remaining firms that specialize in the freshwater variety—most of them in Tennessee, the biggest popularity stronghold for freshwater natural pearls.

But once out of areas where they have long been fished, freshwater pearls exert little of the lure they once did. Maybe that's for the best since production, according to one Tennessee pearl culturer, is less than 1% of what it was 40 years ago in the twilight of meaningful freshwater pearl fishing. So where do the freshwater pearls come from that dealers need to meet resurgent connoisseur demand?

Almost always nowadays they are found on land, not under water.

FOLLOW THE RIVER

Except for one or two dealers who bought out dealer stocks of freshwater pearls after World War II when cultured pearls finally gained aesthetic parity with the natural variety, and still have surpluses of these beauties, freshwater pearls have attracted pitifully few dealers to their cause. And no wonder. Because few jewelers consider them anything more than curiosities, and few consumers have seen them, freshwater pearls take both flair and fortitude to sell.

But before you can sell them, you have to find them, a task that requires cunning and stamina. A tyro with no backlog from the glory days of this gem has to track down old collections and stray estate pieces in obscure backwater towns all over the United States and Mexico. That means leaving business cards with bankers in pearl river towns and cities, as well as advertising in local newspapers. If the dealer is lucky, freshwater pearl owners will contact him and he can fly down to inspect their goods. If the pearls are worthwhile, negotiations begin, often taking several visits to conclude.

EVALUATING FRESHWATER PEARLS

Quality in freshwater pearls depends on five factors: size, shape, color, luster and cleanliness. Because freshwater pearl production is down precipitously in the last 30 years (at least 20 species of American pearl mussels have died out since 1900 and 20 more are now listed as endangered) and because mussels live shorter lives (due to toxic wastes), U.S. pearl sizes aren't what they used to be. Nowadays, sizes over 6mm in symmetrical and 9mm in baroque (asymmetrical) shapes are considered

AMERICAN FRESHWATER PEARL

large and therefore rare.

Unlike cultured pearls, the predominant shape of freshwater pearls is baroque, comprising at least 95% of the production now and perhaps always. Symmetrical pearls are more apt to be button- or pear-shaped than spherical. Of the baroque shapes, the majority are elongated, resembling bird's wings and dog's teeth. Most prized are what dealers call "classic" shapes, two in particular: the rosebud (a high-domed round to oval pearl with lots of ridges and bumps on the top) and the turtle-back (a turtle-shell shape with a smooth back).

Color in freshwater pearls has the greatest range and variety of any pearl type. Yet 90% of what is found today is white, with some creams and silvers. Far more rare are the blacks, greens, blues, oranges, pinks, purples and lavenders. The most coveted colors are what are known as "fancy colors," usually the pinks, purples and oranges. When judging color, dealers look for overall body color and overtone. It is hard to completely separate color in pearls from their luster, or basic brightness. Technically speaking, luster is the amount of white light from the pearl reflected back to the eye. At its best, luster resembles "a drop of mercury."

Don't confuse luster with orient, the amount of iridescence observed when a pearl is moved under the light. Orient is usually stronger in natural pearls because they have the requisite depth and transparency of nacre (the substance secreted by a mollusk to make a pearl) to allow for the light penetration and breakup needed to produce iridescence. Orient is strongest in baroque natural shapes where surface irregularities heighten it.

Last, cleanliness plays a minor role in determining a pearl's value. Ideally, a pearl surface should be free of discolorations, holes, pits, scratches, gouges and the like. Due to rarity, some blemishes are acceptable, especially in large sizes. Fortunately, pearls can sometimes be peeled to remove skin-deep blemishes, but it takes an expert.

Because freshwater pearls are so rare, their prices tend to be higher than the cultured variety. Nevertheless, much freshwater pearl jewelry is still very affordable. Because freshwater pearls are principally baroque, jewelry pieces tend to be free-form, generally using 10k or 14k-gold and occasionally 18k gold and platinum with finer pearls.

CHINESE FRESHWATER PEARL

Quantity kills quality.

As an example, we cite the Shanghai lake district of China, the world's prime producer of freshwater cultured pearls.

To boost harvests of these very popular pearls, most of which resemble Rice Krispies, the Chinese government has turned pearl farming there (and elsewhere throughout the country) into something of a numbers game with growers paid purely by pearl weight, not worth. U.S. dealers who buy direct from the Chinese say this weight-over-worth policy has worked to swell output, currently estimated at between 75 and 80 tons annually—but at the expense of top grades. Only a decade ago, better goods accounted for a far more substantial share of overall production. Now they make up, some dealers insist, less than 10% of the country's annual pearl crop. And the percentage is shrinking fast.

"I'm seriously worried about the future of quality pearls from China," says a New York pearl importer who regularly travels to China. He isn't the only dealer with such concern.

THE BIG SHELL OUT

In the name of numbers, Chinese pearl farmers switched from the slow-grow sankaku to the fast-grow kurasu mussel during the late 1970s. Use of the kurasu mussel—which one importer estimates now accounts for 80% of Chinese freshwater pearl production—has cut cultivation time from 36 to as little as 12 months.

But abbreviated growing cycles take a heavy toll in terms of pearl beauty. Nearly all kurasu pearls lack the smooth, lustrous surfaces of their sankaku counterparts. Instead, they are wrinkled and dull, often severely so. Shorter shell life also contributes to a marked decline in production of symmetrical shapes. "The Chinese are harvesting, for the most part, between 12 and 18 months," says a Tennessee-based pearl farmer. "Your chances of getting symmetrical shapes are much better if you leave the pearl at least two years to grow."

This isn't to say that shorter growing cycles are the sole reason for Chinese pearl quality problems. Overcrowding of some lakes and ponds starves mussels of necessary nutrients to make fine pearls. And the comparative lack of Chinese pearl culturing know-how compounds the situation. "For 17 cents an hour, you're not going to find technicians who know the niceties of pearl cultivation," the Tennessee pearl culturer declares.

Learning those niceties is the key to the future of the Chinese pearl industry. Despite experiments cross-implanting the tissue of the kurasu

CHINESE FRESHWATER PEARL

into the sankaku mussel for more shapely, less afflicted pearl growth, many Chinese pearl technicians lack the profound sensitivity and skill—traits their Japanese counterparts possess—to make these experiments in pearl improvement succeed. "How can you produce a beautiful pearl if you don't know the correct way to lay in the mantle tissue that serves as its nucleus?" the Tennessee pearl man asks.

Proper insertion of mantle tissue is essential for decent freshwater pearls. Unlike Japanese akoya and South Sea saltwater cultured pearls, Chinese freshwater pearls contain no shell-bead nucleus to force spherical or, at least, symmetrical growth. Only sections of tissue from sister mussels are used, sometimes as many as 50 to a mussel, but usually closer to 25. As nacre forms around tissue, it does so in freer style, taking a range of shapes from roundish to rice, depending on the way the tissue is first implanted and then shielded from disturbance.

THE SHANGHAI/BIWA CONNECTION

China's lack of sophistication with regard to pearl technology, coupled with its sheer-volume philosophy, has put the country in a bind. At least 80% of the country's yearly pearl harvests are rice pearls, 16-inch strands of which are readily available for ridiculously little in Hong Kong and Taiwan. This abundance of low-grade material only reinforces China's image as a second-class pearl power. But even her best off-round and symmetrical pearls in 7mm sizes are going for bargain-basement prices—even with fetching natural pink colors.

Yet many of these same pearls command three to five times more in Japan where they are sometimes sold as pearls from that island's famed Lake Biwa, an area so ravaged by pollution that the pearl-mussel mortality rate is reported running at 60% to 70%. Within a year or so, production there may stop altogether. Nevertheless, given the large numbers of pearls that continue to be sold as Biwa in origin, few jewelers would guess that the lake is a mollusk death trap.

Statements that pearls from China's Lake Shanghai (or any other Chinese lake for that matter) come from Japan's Lake Biwa are "clearly deceptive and violate the law," says Joel Windman, general counsel of the Jewelers Vigilance Committee, New York. Yet some dealers here and abroad rationalize such misrepresentations by arguing that Japanese high-tech enhancements of Chinese pearls (including bleaching and dyeing) make them, in effect, a Japanese product.

That's stretching things. Nevertheless, many dealers who reject calling Chinese freshwater pearls Biwa have no qualms about labeling them

CHINESE FRESHWATER PEARL

as "Biwa-type" or "Biwa-like." One pearl industry promoter thinks this is equally wrong. "It's deceptive to make an origin term like 'Biwa' into a generic term," he says. "I have never seen a Chinese freshwater pearl equal in quality to the Japanese variety. Use of 'Biwa-type' makes it seem the only difference between the two is geographical." Users of such terms say there is a very strong resemblance between the best Chinese freshwater and Biwa pearls— so strong, in fact, that it takes an expert to tell them apart.

According to one of those experts, Japanese look-alike pearls from China, a decided minority of that country's production, are principally ones known in the trade as flats. "They're similar to Biwa," he explains, "but with one important difference: The Chinese pearls are only flat on one side."

Thankfully, the confusion of Chinese with Japanese pearls affects a relatively small percentage of Chinese freshwater pearls. However, with Japanese freshwater production in big trouble, the Chinese have perhaps their greatest opportunity of the past 20 years to upgrade their overall image as a pearl producer or, at least, restore some of its former luster. But given the technology gap between the Chinese and the Japanese, this will be difficult. The Chinese have some catching up to do.

Yet it's highly doubtful that the Japanese, the most logical choice for technical assistance, will be open to any type of pearl pacts with the Chinese. They remember all too well how they were ejected from Burma after helping to make that country's pearl farms among the finest in the world. Nevertheless, the Chinese have tried several times to interest the Japanese in joint venture pearl farming, always without success. "The Chinese are caught in a severe bind," the Tennessee pearl culturer observes. "During Mao's Cultural Revolution, the government closed nearly all the universities and pretty much deprived a whole generation of higher education. Just how far can China go it alone as a pearl power without, for example, marine biologists?"

CONCH PEARL

What's in a name? Not much when it comes to conch pearls, the Caribbean's contribution to mollusk-made gems. Gemologists treat this name with so little respect that it might as well be an alias.

First of all, the name isn't pronounced "conch," but "conk" (as in honk).

Second, and far more serious, the gem isn't even a pearl. Oh sure, it's got the same basic chemicals—aragonite and calcite—as the oyster pearl. But the ratio between them is so different that the outcome can't be called nacre, although it too is a calcium carbonate—just like an oyster pearl. Besides lacking nacre, the conch pearl grows in a continuous manner (concretion) while the oyster pearl forms in layers.

Okay, if it isn't a pearl proper, then what is it? According to Archie Curtis, a pearl specialist at the Gemological Institute of America in Santa Monica, Calif., it is now called a "calcareous concretion."

Sorry we asked.

"I know the term isn't very romantic," he adds, faintly apologetic, "but the gemologist's job is accuracy."

Maybe so. But until the late 19th century, gemologists allowed romance to take precedence over reality. It is only around 1900 that they start becoming somewhat prissy about pearl nomenclature, objecting in books and articles to according the conch pearl full pearl status.

Ever since, the conch pearl has been considered a bastard pearl—deprived of species membership because of what some say is a silly technicality: growth in the wrong kind of shell.

But it's no laughing matter to gemologists. Around 1900, defenders of the then-emerging new pearl orthodoxy, one of them the great German gemologist Max Bauer, started to argue that conch pearls weren't pearls as such because they came from a shell that lacked a mother-of-pearl layer—something considered essential for the soft, prismatic color effect (also known as "orient") seen in true pearls.

Later generations of gemologists have been even less charitable with the name conch pearl. "No gem identification for a conch 'pearl' will ever leave GIA's labs described as a pearl," Curtis declares.

Nevertheless, the trade at large can be excused for taking a softer line toward these very rare, lovely and coveted gems.

SNAIL VERSUS OYSTER GROWN

Ninety years ago, when natural, noncultured pearls were the norm, the trade often broadly defined a pearl as any organic gem grown by a shell animal to protect itself from an irritation—usually a piece of shell or a parasite (but never, incidentally, the proverbial grain of sand). Hence

CONCH PEARL

it didn't matter if the mollusk was an oyster (bivalve) or snail (univalve). In the case of univalves, the No. 1 pearl producer was, and still is, the great conch (Strombus gigas), a large marine snail found throughout the Caribbean.

Because the conch's meat was a delicacy, and its beautiful shell equally popular as a garden ornament, tens of millions were gathered annually. In roughly 1,000 of these shells, reports the greatest book on pearls ever written, George Kunz's and Charles Stevenson's 1908 masterpiece, "The Book of the Pearl," pearls were found embedded in the conch's meat. If sufficiently large, lustrous and beautiful, the authors continue, these pearls could fetch up to $5,000 in retail stores.

Today, the chances of discovering a pearl in a conch shell, says Susan Hendrickson, a noteworthy collector of conch pearls who works for the Black Hills Institute of Geological Research, Hill City, S.D., are the same as in Kunz's day—one in 10,000 to 15,000. But since conch populations have been practically decimated in some areas (including Florida where fishing for them is now illegal), and since conch pearl culturing has never succeeded, the number of pearls found yearly is far less, perhaps 200 tops, most from the Bahamas.

It is ironic that a pearl found so close to America is so little known here, especially when it is a coveted connoisseur item throughout Europe and the Middle East. In fact, two determined collectors, one European and the other Saudi Arabian, battled the price of a pink 17-carat symmetrically oval conch pearl to just under $12,000 (around $700 per carat) at a Paris auction in the fall of 1984.

Admittedly, that's a stratospheric price for a conch pearl. But Hendrickson's remarkable 3.06-carat conch pearl shown here was, the last we heard of it a few years back, sold for $500 per carat—$1,500 total. Specialists in exotic pearls say the price would be far higher now.

PINK, WITH FLAMES

For the most part, pearls found in conchs are tiny seed pearls. Those worthy of use in jewelry tend to be symmetrical in shape, generally oblong, far more often than baroque. Occasionally they are spherical. Impressive sizes have been found. In fact, Sotheby's in Geneva tried unsuccessfully to sell a 100-carat tan conch pearl a few years ago.

The principal determinant of value for a conch pearl is its color. Although most tend to be brown, beige or ivory, enough are pink for these pearls to have been known as "pink pearls" in the trade circa 1900. Today, as then, collectors expect these pearls to be anywhere from deep

CONCH PEARL

rose red (in smaller sizes) or salmon orange to eyeshadow pink.

What's more, collectors want to see a unique mottled-color effect called "flame structure." This is the snail-pearl counterpart to orient in oyster pearls and appears, in Bauer's words, as "delicate white wavy lines, like the most beautiful pink velvet." The conch pearl shown here perfectly embodies Bauer's description.

Like the shells from which they come, conch pearls have a tendency to fade if exposed to prolonged sunlight. So Hendrickson advises wearing them mostly as a "night gem." This is the only caveat about conch pearls different from those given for oyster pearls.

Once a popular item in America, conch pearls may be on the comeback trail. In 1985, Harry Winston Inc., a name which stands for jewelry opulence, created a magnificent conch pearl and diamond necklace with accompanying conch pearl and diamond earrings. "That's just about the highest form of recognition the conch pearl has received in 75 years," Hendrickson says.

JAPANESE AKOYA PEARL

According to Islamic mysticism, the first thing God created was a tablet on which was recorded every event that would ever take place until Judgment Day. Next, God created a perfect sphere some 70,000 leagues in size with 70,000 tongues to sing his praises. He turned the sphere into a mighty ocean from which all life emerged.

Both the tablet and sphere were made of pearl.

Given such veneration for this organic gem, it is hardly surprising that for centuries men dreamed of systematically forcing oysters to grow more pearls—rather than leave production to the highly selective whims of nature. Experimentation with pearl culturing is recorded as far back as the 12th century.

But it wasn't until seven centuries later, in the 1890s, that two Japanese working independently of each other discovered a workable pearl culturing method, one that took until 1908 to perfect. Using this method, Japanese pearl farmer Kokichi Mikimoto, to pearls what Henry Ford is to cars, introduced the Japanese akoya (meaning: cultured) pearl in 1919. For years thereafter, Mikimoto was a one-man De Beers for pearls, his farms credited with at least 75% of the gem's entire world production.

Today, the cultured pearl market has many kingpins. But it is still tightly controlled by the Japanese, whose akoya-variety harvests account for at least 70% of annual pearl production. Almost all of the remaining 30%, much of it from China and the South Seas, is also cultured in one way or another. Yet purists still consider the cultured pearl a manmade gem.

It isn't. True, the pearl is provoked by man, not nature, when live mollusk mantle tissue, along with a sizeable spherical bead nucleus cut from a Mississippi drainage area mussel shell, are inserted into the oyster. But such intervention alone doesn't make the cultured pearl nonnatural, not when you realize that pearl farmers think themselves lucky when 20% of their implanted oysters grow pearls. If all goes well, a big "if" left largely to nature, the implanted mantle tissue will shortly envelop the bead and that will, in turn, trigger layerings of nacre (mother of pearl) around the nucleus by the host oyster. Several hundred layerings are needed for a decent pearl, a thousand or more for top grades.

Unfortunately, decent nacre buildup takes at least three years. Well into the 1950s, says one New York pearl importer, "three-year growing times were still the norm in Japan and four- and five-year cycles common." To meet unprecedented demand in this decade, average pearl growing times, already trimmed to two years, were whittled further to 18 months, even less. The end result: a highly predictable and well-publicized flood of substandard pearls. As their meager nacre coatings wore off, consumer confidence wore out. Now, say dealers, the deluge is end-ing and the Japanese are pledged to quality again.

PROBLEMATIC PROMISE
Pearl culturing standards aren't what they used to be. Greed is as much to blame as nature. Besides abbreviated growing times, the tank-bred pearl oysters used nowadays are less hardy than those once taken direct from the sea. Overcrowding waters with these oysters only weakens them more by putting a greater drain on nutrients. Add to this a typhoon or two, as well as increased pollution, and the chances of a banner pearl crop furl even more. No wonder the Japanese talk seriously about transferring the pearl culturing process from the sea to the laboratory. It is hoped that with genetic engineering techniques pearls can one day be grown in test tubes rather than oysters.

Meanwhile, the Japanese must contend with conditions far less con-ducive to growing the lustrous cultured pearls that nearly 70 years ago so easily stole the thunder of the natural variety. Those pearls required great skill to identify by eye—so much so that in 1930, when it became evident that many cultured pearls were being sold as natural, steep prices for the latter crashed 85%. Only after World War II were X-rays employed to tell the difference. Before then, dealers had to learn how to use their own eyes to tell them apart. One New York natural pearl expert even tells a Zen-like story of the day he finally developed, after years of try-ing, "the sixth sense" to distinguish natural from cultured pearls.

Don't get us wrong. Magnificent cultured pearls are still produced. But now when quantity is stressed over quality some connoisseurs fear that the truly fabulous akoya pearl may one day be as rare as the natural pearl it replaced.

The Japanese defend their recent growing practices by saying they were only meeting a seemingly insatiable demand for low-end pearl strands. That demand intensified when the dollar began to plunge against the yen in September 1985 and retailers felt constrained to stay within certain inflexible price boundaries. To their credit, the Japanese tried to hold the line on prices, and today continue to absorb a hefty share of continued dollar devaluations. Yet the temptation to cut cor-ners is undeniable. How else does one explain the fact that tens of thousands of reject pearls, ordinarily barred from export by Japan's pearl inspection office, have made their way to transshipping centers such as Hong Kong and, from there, to the United States and Europe?

JAPANESE AKOYA PEARL

U.S. pearl importers assure us that dumping here of pearls-in-name-only is about over. But newspapers still carry ads, many from reputable jewelers, of "magnificent" 6-6½mm pearl strands in fashionable 18-inch lengths for $100 to $200. "I couldn't afford to sell my commercial strands at wholesale for such prices," complains one importer.

THE 4CS FOR PEARLS
Weakened public confidence in pearls may have a beneficial side. Following De Beers' lead, dealers now seriously entertain a pearl quality advertising and public education program similar to the very successful 4Cs campaign for diamonds. One reason the campaign has not been launched is that some dealers fear it may stimulate demand for top-grade strands at a time when production of them is declining rapidly and prices for those available are more than the vast majority of U.S. jewelers want to pay. "If such a program had been proposed in the early 1980s," says a New York pearl importer, "it would have been more welcomed."

Nevertheless, a growing number of dealers advocate some sort of pearl beauty campaign that would make price and quality comparisons easier for retailers and consumers. Such an effort, it is believed, could help to prevent a flood of substandard pearls similar to that of the mid-1980s by giving jewelers the means to demonstrate quality differences to customers. What's more, pearl quality is relatively easy to communicate, especially since American color and shape preferences fall into very narrow ranges: cream-rose to pinkish colors and round shapes almost exclusively. "The point is this," says one advocate of a 4Cs program for pearls, "let people see for themselves the cut-offs in quality for strands. Junk pearls only look good in a vacuum."

TAHITIAN BLACK PEARL

Once a month, a boat brings provisions to a tiny Pacific atoll called Marutea in the outlying southeastern portion of French Polynesia, better known as Tahiti. This is the only contact with the outside world the island's 50 or so inhabitants have.

That's because the island is private property, bought by Hong Kong businessman Robert Wan in 1986 from Frenchman Jean-Claude Brouillet. How did Brouillet come into possession of a South Sea island in the first place?

The Polynesian government sold Marutea to Brouillet in 1974 on the condition that he start an industry there. Brouillet chose pearl farming. Every August since 1976, workers at the island's lagoon fishery have harvested, on average, some 25,000 wearable natural-color black cultured pearls that when round range in size from 9½ to 13mm, and are occasionally as large as 16mm.

Although marketers of Marutea's pearl crop have claimed that the island is responsible for about 70% of the world's annual black pearl production, specialists in South Sea pearls say its contribution is probably closer to 40%. The lower figure makes sense since Wan owns at least one other farm as large as the one he bought from Brouillet and is said to hold controlling interests in a few more sprinkled throughout Polynesia.

But the fact that so many jewelers believe in Marutea's disproportionate importance is a tribute to one New York South Sea pearl dealer, who almost single-handedly popularized Brouillet's Tahitian blacks in return for the exclusive rights to market them.

However, now that the Marutea farm is part of Wan's black pearl conglomerate this dealer may have to share the spotlight he has had to himself for more than a decade. "I don't see how one person can handle all that production," says a fellow South Sea pearl dealer. Another pearl dealer who has long sold Tahitian black pearls tells us he has already been approached by Wan to share in future marketing. But even with a bigger cast of players, the Tahitian black pearl market will remain fundamentally the same.

ISLANDS OF PEARL PLENTY

The Marutea black pearl farm is the best-known of the dozens of large and small South Seas black pearl culturing ventures, most of them found in Tahiti (hence the name, Tahitian black pearl). Marutea, like most island pearl farm operations, is remote, located 1,000 miles from Papeete, the capital of Tahiti. Here Marutea's black beauties are flown—a seven-

TAHITIAN BLACK PEARL

hour trip by air—after harvesting and grading, to be handed over to their American and European distributors.

With at least 50% of total cultured black pearl production coming from Wan-owned or Wan-controlled farms, the market has little to fear in the way of turbulence. The only threats are from nature. But except for hurricanes and such, things are just as you'd expect them in the South Seas: smooth and tranquil.

Nevertheless, there are those who wish pearl farming on Marutea and all other Polynesian islands would take on more of the hustle and bustle it has in Japan. That's not likely, though, for a number of reasons.

LONGER SHELL LIFE

Black pearls are produced by a black-lipped oyster found throughout Micronesia (a vast South Sea island complex that includes French Polynesia). As with the far more plentiful Japanese variety, Tahitian pearl culturing consists of inserting mantle tissue from a sister oyster plus a bead-nucleus, made entirely of processed Mississippi River system clamshell, into the oyster, then waiting until the oyster covers it with a substantial layer of secretion called nacre.

Although culturing techniques are the same, philosophies of pearl growing are different in Japan and Tahiti. To boost pearl production, Japanese often implant oysters with two or more nuclei. Indeed, if you are buying Japanese cultured pearls that are 6mm or less in size, you should assume they came from multiple dwelling pearl oysters.

In Polynesia, however, pearl farmers stick doggedly to a one-pearl-per-oyster policy, even though the South Sea oyster used is much larger than its Japanese counterpart. This is the way it's always been there and, say producers, is meant to stay. One reason for the single nucleus policy is that Tahiti is famous for large pearls. Multiple implantations would increase production—but at the expense of greater sizes.

Tahitian pearl growers also depart from the Japanese emphasis in recent years on shorter and shorter growing times. As far as we know, every oyster harvested has spent at least two years in the water. But by taking growing times to such lengths, Tahitian pearl farmers sacrifice a good many round pearls. Remember, the longer a pearl sits in an oyster, the greater its chances of shifting position and growing unevenly. Hence the overwhelming majority of Tahitian pearls are baroque. In fact, the New York dealer confesses, production of round pearls on Marutea is only 3%, vastly below the percentage of Japan. Nevertheless, he isn't complaining. He notes that baroque shapes are very popular in Europe. And

TAHITIAN BLACK PEARL

since prices paid for top-quality large round black pearls in graduated strands can reach $1 million at retail, he feels more than compensated for ultra-limited round harvests.

In any case, the emphasis on quality over quantity throughout Polynesia has been a big selling point. For example, each year, usually between April and June, Japanese technicians on Marutea implant some 60,000 oysters. Two, sometimes three years later, they are harvested, generally, says the dealer, with at least a 40% success rate.

Their long incubation period results in a layer of nacre thicker than that of most Japanese pearls. Many Japanese pearls sold abroad have a nacre thickness well under 1mm due to their shorter time in the sea. The New York dealer's pearls, on the other hand, generally boast a minimum nacre thickness of 2mm.

As with white pearls, there are definite standards for excellence in black pearls. Foremost is color, which runs from light gray to dark gray, often with bluish, peacock-green and eggplant-green overtones. At present, high-luster peacock greens and some gun-metal grays are the most coveted colors.

Second in importance is cleanliness, for which dealers use a grading system that starts at A, spotless, moves to F, then down to SP1, SP2 and SP3 (to indicate various degrees of spotting).

Luster, or surface shine, is more subjective. But the best black pearls have a kind of high-polish surface, reminiscent, in ways, of a ball bearing. Last, but not least, comes shape, ranked in desirability as follows: round, pear, semiround, drop, button, baroque and rejection. The New York dealer says he has a very small percentage of rejection pearls. "The oyster either produces or it doesn't."

BURMA PERIDOT

In 1962, just before a military takeover of Burma and an abrupt closing off of the country to Westerners, a New York cutter bought a large selection of very fine to superb 20- to 40-carat peridots there for $1.50 per carat.

Nearly three decades later, the only Burmese peridot he can find is decent but far from great—yet the price asked of him is 100 times that of Burma's best before the country was shut off from the world. And, mind you, this is the cost to a seasoned haggler in Thailand, the next-door haven for Burmese gems. The lapidary says he can't begin to figure out what consumers would have to pay today for the kind of top-grade material in sizes between 20 and 40 carats that he bought in 1962.

But even if he could, all the cutter's estimates would be moot. "I can't find any goods," he complains. "Not in Asia or America."

The paucity of fine large peridot comes, as is so often the case in the jewelry world, just when this gem is capturing lots of attention. Peridot's status as the August birthstone, its pleasing green and its bargain price relative to its extreme scarcity in top grades make it possible for dealers who carry this gem to sell all the fine-specimen large stones they can rustle up from estates, auctions or each other.

"I wish I could lay my hands on enough large, clean and well-cut peridots to fill the calls I keep getting for it," says a New York gem importer. "The market wants peridot, but not the kind dealers can provide."

What they can provide are smaller stones, generally under 3 carats, with a green highly reminiscent of a 7Up bottle—most of them from Arizona where peridot is plentiful. But it's the wrong kind of plenty. Because America produces almost no large stones, peridot is rarely seen in solitaire or center stone jewelry. Rather, it's used most frequently to lend accent or create a multi-color effect. It is highly doubtful that most jewelers have seen, let alone sold, a true connoisseur's peridot. And unless a mineralogical miracle occurs, their chances of seeing one will become even slimmer.

SOURCE SPOTS

Peridot, which is a member of the olivine family, depends on body mass for color beauty. Because large stones have become so rare, the green for which this gem has for centuries been praised—a hue one cutter likens to "late-summer grass"—is seldom seen these days.

So prized was this saturate green that one of antiquity's favorite compliments to peridot was to mistake it for emerald. A few jewelry historians are now convinced that some, maybe all, of the emeralds Cleopatra was

BURMA PERIDOT

famous for wearing were peridots from an island off Egypt. One famous large gem adorning the shrine of the Three Holy Kings in the cathedral at Cologne was for centuries believed to be an emerald—and only identified as peridot late in the last century.

Alas, this take-me-for-emerald green is almost never encountered in peridots under 10 carats. To find stones with such color, one has a choice of two source spots where, for various reasons, production has been at, or headed toward, a virtual standstill in recent years: Egypt and Burma. (Norway is also an occasional producer.)

The oldest and most celebrated source is St. John's Island (also known as Zabargad or Zebirget) in the Red Sea, some 34 miles off the coast of Egypt. Although this deposit was worked for thousands of years, its exact whereabouts became something of a mystery for several centuries until being rediscovered in 1905. Shortly thereafter, production resumed, peaked by the late 1930s and tapered off to practically nothing in 1958 when the mines were nationalized. Although parcels of St. John's peridot still come on the market now and then, it is not known if this is new or old material. Most assume it is the latter. That is why St. John's Island has a mystique among connoisseurs for its peridot that is akin to that of Kashmir, a presumably played-out source in northern India, for sapphire.

No one is sure if Burma has also played itself out as a peridot source. Before a coup d'etat in 1962 that left the country a socialist totalitarian state controlled by its army, Burma was a thriving gem producer, principally in its north-central Mogok district not too far off from Mandalay. Nearly 30 years later, Burma, like most of Asia's socialist strongholds, is an economic shambles—so poor and repressed that massive anti-government protests finally erupted in 1988. Given these facts, it would probably be safe to say that politics are the reason Burma no longer can be counted on for peridot.

Obviously, the country produces some gems. But mining is clandestine and most goods are passed on to the outside world through a rather elaborate network of smugglers. Although some intrepid Westerners still venture into Burma to search for goods, most find it safer to pursue their quest in next-door Thailand, the chief conduit for Burmese contraband.

Most peridots dealers see in Thailand are tinkered-with roughs that have crude tables and bottom facets but are a long way from being finished gems. "The partially-cut peridots that we buy generally must lose another 50% [of their weight]," a New York lapidary says. "But at least

BURMA PERIDOT

the table lets you get a good idea of the color inside the stone." But even peridots which supposedly have been fully cut by the Thais often need trimming to unlock more brilliance. Since trimming adds to the per-carat cost of the finished stone, dealers less keen on perfection settle for somewhat flabby peridots.

CONNOISSEUR QUIBBLES
The peerless reputation of Burma's ruby, jade and cultured pearl has rubbed off on the country's peridot, helping to heighten collector interest in it and make it worthwhile for dealers to search out specifically Burmese specimens. Nevertheless, traditionalists deny Burma peridot full parity with the Egyptian variety. While acknowledging its ideal color, they note that Burmese material is usually less clean and hence less brilliant than that from St. John's. "Burma stones tend to have carbon spots and a 'rain-like' texture in them that keeps a good number of them from being gems," the New York cutter says.

Gemologists variously describe this brownish, sometimes grayish texture as "dust" or "pepper." But whatever it's called, it can impart a sleepy or hazy appearance—not to mention an objectionably dark olive color—to a stone. Although specks are not always visible to the naked eye, you'll probably see them if you look at a stone at 3x or 10x magnification with a loupe. For this reason, clarity is an extremely important factor when buying peridot.

When shopping for peridot, keep in mind that this stone is relatively soft (6½ on the Mohs hardness scale) and should be spared rugged, regular wearing if mounted in rings. When the stone is bought loose, remind the setter that peridot is highly sensitive to rapid temperature changes. Many peridots have been destroyed at the bench because pieces containing them were dipped in a cold solution after soldering. One other caveat concerning jewelry repair: Peridots can lose their polish if they come in contact with commonly used hydrochloric or sulfuric acid.

RUBELLITE

After East African chrome tourmaline—a rare green gem which, at its best, can double for fine tsavorite or even emerald—rubellite is the most prized and expensive member of the very broad tourmaline group. Although the name suggests that it is a red tourmaline, that's mostly wishful thinking.

Thinking that may finally be becoming a thing of the past.

More often than not, rubellites tend to be too violet to be considered red in the sense that a ruby is red. "Reddish" would probably be more accurate. Not that rubellites don't on occasion look like rubies. We photographed one such ruby stand-in from Madagascar for this essay. And recently we were shown a suite of Brazilian stones from the famous but fizzled Ouro Fino deposit that were, in the words of their owner, "red, red, red." He meant that they did not have strong overtones of violet or, as often happens, heavy interference from brown.

This isn't to say that basically violetish rubellite isn't deserving of a gem name that hints at red. The same dealer showed us scores of reddish-plum and cranberry-color rubellites, mostly from Africa, that struck us as sensational. Nevertheless, the red in all these stones would have to be described more as a rich highlight or overtone than a basic hue. And, in fact, the owner of these stones only regarded as true rubellites his tiny private stock of ripe-strawberry-color stones from Brazil.

Measured against this strawberry-color ideal, one has to conclude that rubellite is one of the more elastic gem names. The term covers a wide gamut of shades from violet well into pink—with ruby red in a narrow mid-range. Complicating matters further is a controversy involving the transition point between rubellite and pink tourmaline. To us, the term rubellite, whether referring to red or violet stones, connotes medium to dark tones and fairly saturate colors. Most pink tourmalines aren't deep enough in tone or color to qualify.

This nomenclature controversy takes on new relevance now that rubellite is thought of as much as a pink stone as a ruby substitute, the result of pink's current popularity as a fashion staple. We won't try to settle this controversy here. But it seems far less like stretching terms to sell what is essentially a reddish-violet gem as pink rather than as red.

CLARITY PROBLEMS
Even when rubellites qualify as true ruby stand-ins from a color standpoint, chances are great they won't be as clean as kindred-color rubies. Due to its crystal structure, most rubellite is imperfect to some degree.

RUBELLITE

Yet the fact that rubellite is generally included has not stopped it from attracting a wide gem collector following. Jewelers and consumers have been considerably less tolerant of the stone's commonly glaring inclusions. "Americans think about colored stones the way they do about diamonds," explains one dealer. "So they expect colored stones to be 4Cs-clean. And that's an expectation rubellite finds hard to meet." For this reason, notes a Brazilian gem specialist, "It is very hard to sell commercial-grade rubellite."

It's equally hard to *buy* top-grade rubellite. Indeed, supplies are so sporadic that when fine goods hit the market American dealers find themselves pitted against, and usually outbid by, Brazilian and German firms willing to pay sky-high prices. Thankfully, growing acceptance of medium-toned, moderate-priced violetish African rubellite makes it possible to sell stones that are not eye-clean because the color of these stones either hides inclusions or makes them far less noticeable.

MYSTIQUES OF PLACE
Although rubellite is found in America, Africa and Afghanistan, among other places, easily 75% of present world production comes from Brazil, principally that country's famed Minais Gerais gem mining region. Since rubellite deposits are scattered and most of them short-lived, color is variable and generalizations about it are hard to make. The most recent source of superb Brazilian rubellite was Ouro Fino. At their best, Ouro Fino stones tended to be a strawberry red. More typically, the mine's better stones were a deeper cranberry red. For the most part, however, stones we saw exhibited too much purple for our tastes and sometimes even contained brown. So don't start salivating just because a rubellite is purported to be from the legendary but defunct deposit.

That kind of Pavlovian response over tourmaline origin would be more justified these days for stones from Madagascar. This African country has earned a reputation in recent years for producing rich-red stones that not only evoke ruby in general but Burma ruby in particular. Indeed, it is currently assumed that the finer rubellites one sees are from Africa. That's quite a tribute to a continent that was hardly known to jewelers for its rubellite five years ago.

HIGH-TECH HIGH JINX
In recent years, dealers have been seeing more fine plum and cranberry-red rubellites than ever before. The abundance stems from the fact that rubellite has joined topaz as a frequently irradiated gem. Irradiation con-

RUBELLITE

verts near-colorless and shallow pink stones to deep-hued beauties with intense pink and purplish colors. When dealers first became aware of this fact in the early 1980s, the rubellite market crashed. But after dealers realized irradiation-produced rubellite colors were permanent, and stones subjected to this process posed no health hazards if stored until residual radioactivity grew unmeasurable, prices stabilized and have since risen steadily.

Although rubellite is commonly irradiated, there is virtually no chance that the market will ever be as inundated with bombarded tourmaline as it has been with irradiated topaz. That's because tourmaline is simply nowhere near as plentiful as topaz. Given the scarcity of rubellite relative to topaz, the gem's prices recovered fairly quickly from the initial shock when it was discovered that goods were being bombarded.

But another shock may be on the way. Limited quantities of low-grade fissure-laden rubellites are both being bombarded to improve color and impregnated with high-tech plastic resins that hide their cracks and spiff up overall appearance. So far these stones are still being sold in a reputable manner by those who are treating them. But if the past is any guide to the future, eventually some unscrupulous dealer may try to pass off these clearly adulterated stones as what they're not: equal in status and value to natural or merely bombarded rubellite.

As worrisome, few dealers even seem to know that this two-step impregnation/irradiation process exists, although some dealers suspect something different about many of the rubellites they are seeing. Many note a certain unmistakable brownness in stones. Others complain of color dullness. Since brown is a color-duller, they might just be describing the same characteristic. In any case, the question remains: Is what they are sensing a sign of irradiation as they suspect or, perhaps, impregnation and irradiation combined? It's a question dealers will have to grapple with soon—and whose answer they will have to share with jewelers and their public.

BURMA RUBY

Dealers old enough to remember the golden age nearly 30 years back when Burma ruby was so plentiful there was no need to sell any other variety have had to make a painful peace with stones from substitute sources, mainly Thailand and, more recently, East Africa.

Those too young to remember are more skeptical. Were the best Burma rubies of yesteryear really so superior? Or were they, like so many other bygones, an over-sentimentalized fantasy?

To decide which, *Modern Jeweler's* yuppie-generation gem market specialist spent a couple of days making cold-eyed comparisons of better-to-fine classification Burma and Thai rubies, hundreds of carats of them, ranging from melee to 5-carat sizes.

His conclusion was, as traditionalists assured him it would be, that Burma ruby has no peer. Despite color-bolstering from heat treatment, Thai rubies generally flunk side-by-side savorings with Burma goods.

Burma ruby's vast aesthetic edge became most apparent during a visual onslaught in the office of a New York gem importing company. There one of the firm's principals brought out box after box of better-to-fine Burmese and Thai material for our man's inspection. Able to pit scores of Burma and Thai stones against each other, he could see amazing, often overwhelming, differences in color and appearance.

Although difficult to put into words, the final difference came down to "sex appeal." For the most part, the Burma stones had a softer, slightly pinker red with lighter tones. The Thai stones, by comparison, seemed harder in color, darker in tone and prone to annoying grays and browns. What's more, when held at a distance, the color of the Burma stones seemed more pronounced.

Admittedly, all of this is subjective. Quite possibly, some of the stones designated "Burmese" hailed from the increasingly important ruby belt running across Afghanistan and Pakistan. Others may have been pretenders from Kenya, Tanzania and even Thailand itself. Nevertheless, the overall experience made as profound an impression as any in this writer's many years of jewelry market coverage.

Gemologists say such exalted feelings about Burma ruby are hardly surprising. Nature has showered some distinct blessings on this breed.

THE FLUORESCENCE FACTOR

If no longer entirely synonymous with a specific origin, the term "Burma" is still synonymous with ideal beauty in a ruby. Whether a rich solemn intricate red called "pigeon's blood" or a more bubbly pinkish color called "cherry red," Burma rubies at their best have a distinctive glow, especially in broad daylight. This glow, explains eminent gemologist Robert Crowningshield of the Gemological Institute of America, Santa Monica, Calif., is the direct result of fluorescence. When fluorescent stones are struck by ultraviolet rays, a strong component of sunlight, they excite atoms within. This reaction adds extra punch.

Thai rubies almost always lack the vibrancy of their Burmese brethren. They are cursed, Crowningshield continues, with the presence of iron, a trace element that affects color for the worse by adding purple and brown, all the while inhibiting fluorescence. Heating ruby is enough to alter the state of the iron and remove some of the purple and brown. But the process doesn't significantly boost fluorescence. Hence heated Thai rubies still lack what one dealer calls "jazz."

To a generation reared on Thai ruby, however, there is no way to appreciate this missing ingredient. Hard to define unless seen, it makes it even harder to justify the rather hefty price differentials between Burma and Thai rubies. Today, for instance, a very fine 3-carat unheated Burma ruby can easily command about three times its Thai counterpart.

Thankfully, Burma/Thai price differentials narrow as stones get smaller. Very fine all-natural 1-carat Burma rubies currently wholesale for roughly 50% more than very fine 1-carat Thai stones. With fine melee, the Burma premium dwindles to 25%. Considering the desperate disproportion between supplies of Thai and Burma stones, this makes Burmese goods a bargain.

GIVE MY REGARDS TO MOGOK
Ever since Burma's socialist government sealed off the country in 1962, Burma ruby has been an endangered species. But even before its borders closed, mining in the country's principal gem tract at Mogok, in north-central Burma, was in sharp decline.

One of the few American gem dealers alive today to have ever visited Mogok remembers that as of his last visit in 1960, miners were already reworking the tailings of combed-over deposits. "The future of supply was open to question before Burma became off bounds," he says.

This isn't to say that mining has ceased. It is believed to continue, but only in a token and largely clandestine manner. Most of what the West sees in the way of "new" Burma rubies, whether those mostly mediocre stones offered at once-a-year gem auctions in Rangoon or the modicum of far finer pieces smuggled into neighboring Thailand, are probably hoarded goods. The same goes for the majority of Burma

BURMA RUBY

rubies sold in major Asian gem centers such as India, Hong Kong and Singapore. In Europe and America, the market is almost entirely dependent on vintage goods, many from estates.

Given the profusion of heat-treated Burma pretenders, authentication of origin has become as important to gem dealers as authentication of authorship is to art dealers. The job of verifying Burmese origin is difficult, often involving intricate microscope scrutiny, as well as painstaking historical research. Few in the profession of gemology are trained for this work. And, indeed, the field of gemstone origin authentication is in its infancy, presently dominated by two labs, New York's American Gemological Laboratories and Zurich's Gubelin Laboratory, whose findings sometimes conflict.

Since an origin pedigree is now a prerequisite to sale of Burma rubies in the auction and connoisseur markets, sellers will often submit stones to both labs and use the authentication certificate of whichever lab concludes the stone is from Burma. At present, the Gubelin lab in Switzerland is the better-known and preferred. But that doesn't necessarily mean its work is better. To the contrary, American Gemological Laboratories has irked some dealers because it insists on noting whether or not stones, even those from Burma, are heat-treated—a reality for almost all modern-mined rubies. Many in the trade believe that this information should be excluded from origin reports, even though it is clearly required by Federal Trade Commission gem enhancement disclosure rules for the jewelry industry. In any case, indications of heat treatment on an origin certificate for a Burma ruby can prevent it from receiving as much per carat as a stone from the same place that the laboratory has validated as all-natural. But heated or not, a fine Burma stone will be worth far more than its Thailand counterpart.

EAST AFRICAN RUBY

Although East Africa has gained big league status as a producer of newcomer gems such as tsavorite and tanzanite, it is still considered bush league when it comes to traditional stones such as sapphire and emerald.

For sure, the region is rich in these standbys. However, the quality of stones found so far is generally judged inferior to that from other active gem localities such as Burma and Sri Lanka for sapphire, or Colombia and Zambia for emerald.

That leaves ruby, which East Africa mines in abundance, to earn it the respect it craves as a source of stalwart gems. Ruby finds in Kenya have already begun to raise hopes. But no one is ready yet to raise glasses. "It all depends on whether the new deposits prove the rule rather than the exception," says a Seattle dealer who specializes in African gems.

Judging from the number of Thai, German, Israeli and American dealers buying East African ruby rough in Kenya these days, it looks like better grades have become the rule.

"If production stays this good, East African ruby could be on the verge of full acceptance," says another East African gem specialist who lives in Bermuda. "The new production gives Burma and Thailand (the prime sources of ruby) a real run for the money."

What has the newer East African ruby got that older stones from this region lack? And how good does that really make this ruby when compared to that of its Southeast Asian counterparts?

BURMA COLOR, AFRICAN PRICE

East Africa has been producing ruby in bulk since around 1970. Because most of its ruby is heavily included, less than 1% of the rough has been suitable for faceting. In fact, East Africa is known chiefly for cabochon ruby. Even now, with better grades more common, the number of facetable stones is minuscule.

However, what African ruby lacks in clarity, it more than compensates for in color. Indeed, up until 1980, as much as 15% of the output from the famed Longido mine in northern Tanzania was said to be virtually indistinguishable color-wise from medium-to-fine Burmese rubies, the most highly prized specimens of this species in the world.

Most other mines, such as Tanzania's Morogoro mine, produced more characteristic material. "The best pieces of rough always had a killer-red with some pink," the Bermuda-based gem dealer says. "But when you cut them into cabs they usually turned a disappointing purplish color."

EAST AFRICAN RUBY

This purplish (sometimes brownish) red, coupled with the stone's coarse silk and super-numerous inclusions (most notably, liquid-filled cavities), gave the stones a flat, lusterless appearance when cut into cabochons.

Their dull, opaque appearance relegated East African rubies to use in low-end jewelry. As a result, the material was associated primarily with Indian dealers in Jaipur who cut the lion's share of this ruby. Gradually, more and more of it found its way to Thailand, with the very top stones reserved for Germany.

Then in 1984, miners started to unearth far more promising rough. News spread fast, so fast that Israeli and American dealers, among others, quickly flocked to Kenya's two main gem buying centers, Nairobi and Mombassa, to bid on new parcels.

THAI BEAUTIFICATION

East Africa's new ruby proved especially exciting to dealers in Thailand. Operating mostly through European and American agents, syndicates of Thai dealers began buying large quantities of the new material. Recently, in fact, Thais have launched their own ruby mining ventures. Concurrently, there has been much-improved translucency and luster in Kenyan stones. Some in the market are convinced that these stones have been heat treated in Thailand. Others say they are simply the products of new deposits.

Given Thailand's reputation for gem beautification, it is easy to see why dealers would suspect that Kenya's more comely rubies would owe their good looks to ovens. Nevertheless, East African gem specialists insist that most, if not all, of these stones are natural. One of them says many Thai efforts at heating African ruby have failed. One reason: too many inclusions that could explode during the heat-treatment process and damage the stone.

Even so, argue dealers who are convinced the Thais are heating East African ruby, the rewards outweigh the risks. According to one Miami gem importer who has experimented with heat treatment, the color of Kenyan ruby is better than that exhibited by most Thai stones. Only heating, he says, could give such a final color finish.

Second, while "expandable inclusions" do present problems, the new ruby seems to be able to take the heat. "Using expensive, high-temperature ovens run in tightly controlled atmospheric conditions," the Miami dealer explains, "treaters in Thailand, including ourselves, can dissolve most of the coarse silk in the African ruby and produce very translu-

EAST AFRICAN RUBY

cent stones."

These stones, the dealer continues, are so close to Burmese ruby in color and appearance that it pays to heat them. "African ruby is already being sold as Burma material on the Thai/Burma border. And some dealers have not even realized it," he says.

A NICHE OF ITS OWN

Despite the fact that East African ruby is often mistaken for Burmese ruby, it is highly doubtful that it will overtake either Burmese or Thai ruby in its standing among connoisseurs any time soon. Instead, dealers expect it to play an important role in the mass jewelry market, especially in light of the resurgence of cabochon-gem jewelry.

For years, the Italians and, to a lesser extent, the French have been ardent admirers of East African ruby. "They don't mind the fact that it's highly included," the Seattle gem importer says. "They just go for that juicy red color."

Now with cabochon jewelry having made such a dramatic comeback in the United States, dealers here are betting that Americans will become devotees of African ruby too.

"It's a superb bluff stone," one dealer says. "African cabochon rubies give large-size gems with high visual appeal at a very low cost."

As far as color, expect stones with either a fine cherry red tinged with pink or a watermelon-like pinkish red. Stones should not be visibly purple or brown. As important, the stones should hold their color in both incandescent and natural daylight. That's because they are highly fluorescent.

Regarding translucency and clarity, stones should verge on semi-translucency and be partially inclusion-free for up to 3-4mm below the surface when observed under penlight.

Last, stones should not be cut with overly high domes or heavy bottoms. These are purely weight-retention measures that add nothing to the beauty of the stone—only to its price.

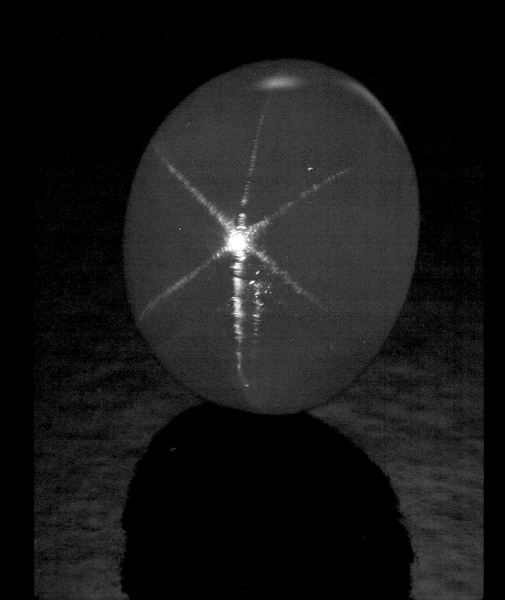

STAR RUBY

If you've ever bought gold or silver bullion, or at least followed the fortunes of these metals, you may recall that for years commodity experts talked of an iron-clad price ratio between these two precious metals of 35:1—favoring gold, of course. Once prices for these metals got too much out of alignment with each other, investment analysts started to fret.

Today, when the gold/silver ratio has spread to as much as 80:1, no one takes the old 35:1 ratio seriously. But it is worth noting that the commodities world long lived by a certain price relationship between the world's two most famous precious metals.

Believe it or not, the gem world once lived by an equally hallowed price ratio—traceable at least as far back as the middle 1600s and still observed at the turn of this century—between its two most coveted faceted gems: diamond and ruby. According to the rule, a 3- to 5-carat ruby was to be priced 10 times higher than its diamond counterpart. Merchants used this ratio as a guide when dickering for stones with dealers.

Although this 10:1 price relationship was rigorously adhered to, there was one major exception made for star ruby. When valuing these stones the ratio was stretched to 12:1.

Today, of course, the fine faceted rubies no longer command anywhere near what star ruby equivalents do. Indeed, faceted rubies no longer fetch what comparable diamonds do—unless they are exceedingly fine and rare stones of bona fide Burma origin. Tastes have changed and with them the precise market price formulas that held sway for centuries.

Mention is made of this long-discarded diamond and ruby pricing equation only to show in what high esteem star ruby was held for hundreds of years. A book published in the late 19th century records jewelry store prices of $3,000 per carat for top-echelon 3-carat star rubies—an impressive sum then, although far below the price of such a stone nowadays. You see, fine star rubies have never been scarcer and hopes for meaningful supply never more futile.

THE BURMA BENCHMARK

Relatively few of the rubies mined today are candidates for cutting into star stones. Most come from Thailand or East Africa and lack the one essential element needed to produce the star effect: rutile.

Why is rutile so important? In corundum, rutile is arranged in densely packed bundles of crisscrossing needles. If plentiful enough, these needles reflect light in a manner that gives the stone a special silken sheen which gemologists call "chatoyancy." When cut in cabochon

STAR RUBY

(domed) form, this light is concentrated into three rays that intersect at right angles to the direction of the needles and resemble a six-legged star. This play of light is called "asterism."

Alas for lovers of star stones, the only rubies with rutile in them are those from Burma and Sri Lanka. But Sri Lankan stones rarely possess the full-bodied red of Burmese stones. Instead, they are mostly a not-too-appreciated purplish-red. As for the few rutile-rich Burmese crystals with fine color worthy of cutting into superb star stones, these will invariably be heat treated to dissolve the rutile and thus make them far more suitable for faceting. The result: a dearth of stellar star rubies.

This dearth does not bother most U.S. gem dealers. Explains one. "I don't get more than a couple of calls a year for this stone."

UNDER ASIAN SKIES
It may seem far-fetched, but some dealers say Americans lack interest in star ruby because these stones look best in the intense sunlight of the Asian countries where they are mined or cut. Dealers who regularly buy rubies in the Orient admit stones viewed there often have a seductive sizzle that disappears in the light of a New York day. Other dealers point out that while the stones do have extra zest in the Oriental light, they wow their beholder under any sky.

Whatever the aesthetics of the matter, price is one irrefutable reason why all but the most well-heeled Americans have shunned these blazing gems. European—and, for that matter, Japanese—jewelry store patrons don't mind the hefty sums asked of them for fine star rubies, especially recently when their currencies have been strong.

Even so, star ruby does not have the popularity anywhere that it did in the 1950s, "the decade of star madness," a dealer recalls. Back then, star ruby was faddish to wear. But fads, as a rule, don't last long. To find an era when star ruby was last a jewelry store staple, you'll have to go back to the 1930s, when star ruby, which has always been more a gent's gem, was seen frequently in men's dress sets, including studs and cuff links. For centuries before, the gem was associated with pomp and circumstance throughout the world. In fact, financier and gem collector J. Pierpont Morgan assembled a major star stone collection which now resides at the American Museum of Natural History in New York.

THE SILVER LINING
For consumers unfamiliar with star ruby, a quick course in aesthetics is in order.

STAR RUBY

To begin with, a fine star will look, in the words of one who has cut them, "pencil sharp—not wide or blurry." What's more, all six legs (or rays) of the star should extend to the base of the cabochon. In addition, the star should be centered and its main ray run the lengthwise direction of the oval. As for the star's color, it should be silvery or milky white with no, or little, bleed-through of red. Be warned, however, that perfect stars are rare, especially in stones with the most desirable Burma-red color.

To visualize this red, think of the color of a Marlboro box—full-blooded with no brown, hopefully no purple and, perhaps, a tiny but tolerable tinge of orange or pink. As stones deviate from this ideal, their value decreases.

Next, consider clarity. Top stones are semi-translucent. Watch out for surface imperfections, usually hair-line fissures that break the surface of the stone and can widen in the course of wearing. Such flaws present problems to cutters because polishing them in the wrong direction only makes them worse.

Last, pay close attention to cutting. Star rubies should be properly proportioned, not too flat on top and not too heavy on the bottom. "If too flat on top, stars seem to swim around too much under a single light," a cutter says. "If too heavy on the bottom, one is paying for concealed weight."

THAI RUBY

Thai ruby still has plenty of detractors in the world gem community. To many old guard dealers, it is a poor substitute for the Burmese variety of this corundum, despite the fact that Burma stopped official gem mining in 1962, leaving the world almost totally dependent on neighboring Thailand and stretches of mine tract just across its Cambodian border. The adjustment to Southeast Asia's other and once-despised variety of ruby has been slow and unenthusiastic.

Granted, Thai stones come in larger sizes and are generally cleaner and brighter. Nevertheless, because connoisseurs usually found them so unforgivably purplish, so unbearably reminiscent of garnet, posh jewelry stores avoided them until necessity finally overcame the retailers' reluctance. Among the longest holdouts: Tiffany's and Van Cleef & Arpels.

Thai dealers were not insensitive to the establishment's lack of esteem for their rubies. But to change its harsh, unaccommodating attitude meant finding the means to change the color of their stones. Some time in the mid- to late-1970s, the Thais discovered a method, using high-heat kilns, and, later, controlled-atmosphere furnaces, that eliminated purple and left their rubies a far more desirable red.

In this way, modern color alchemy broke down longstanding resistance to Thai ruby. Further, as heating was used more and more indiscriminately on ruby, it gradually bred indifference to the fact of treatment. Where once Thai dealers seemed to take care to conceal their art, now they are quite open about it—so much so that they are even subjecting Burma ruby to rather brutal treatment too. This development has many dealers and gemologists concerned. And for good reason.

OVEN POLITICS

Ruby is not the first gem to depend on heat treatment for market acceptability. Aquamarine, citrine and, more recently, tanzanite, to name a few, are largely the products of color enhancement in an oven. In the case of these gems, however, heating created a standard of beauty that otherwise would have been unattainable. Not so with ruby.

"Even with heating, you did not in 999 out of 1,000 cases produce stones that stood up to comparison with the best of Burma," says a New York cutter.

In short, Thai rubies, although boasting vastly better looks, faced no-win comparisons with Burma. The art of Thailand's heat treaters may have been long, but the memories of connoisseurs were longer. However, when Thai dealers began extreme heating of Burma, in addition to Thai

THAI RUBY

stones, treatment obliterated most if not all of the tell-tale internal signs that gemologists use as conclusive evidence of Burma origin. Gem origin specialist Cap Beesley of American Gemological Laboratories in New York calls this process "super frying" and says he is seeing signs of it in an alarming number of stones. "Rubies that your instinct tells you came from Burma are almost completely devoid of the characteristics we once took as proof of our hunches," Beesley says. "As a result, we can't issue confirming documents on them."

Without these documents, Burma stones risk a limbo where they must be sold on the basis of physical appearance alone—color, clarity, cutting and the like—and sacrifice origin-based premiums that take into account their far greater rarity and historical aesthetic supremacy.

Thankfully, there are still many fine unmolested Burma rubies coming into the market from estates and dealers' old stocks whose origin can be authenticated. In fact, it is nearly impossible to sell Burma stones as such today in sizes of 3 carats or more without accompanying origin documents issued by recognized labs such as Gubelin's in Zurich or American Gemological Laboratories. Stones whose papers are in order can command a price at least 100% higher than a look-alike without a positive identification as Burmese. If unpedigreed, a Burma look-alike is presumed to be a heat-treated Thai stone until proven otherwise.

Under 3 carats, however, lab pedigrees don't mean as much. Thai stones have made such inroads that confirmed 3-carat Burma-origin rubies are lucky to command a 50% premium, 1- to 2-carat sizes often only 25% to 30% more. This shrinking Burma-Thai price differential has purists worried. "At this rate, there will soon be price parity," says one cutter.

For the Thais, as well as many gem dealers worldwide, parity would be welcome. They resent the fact that mediocre Burma stones can fetch as much or more than better-looking Thai stones purely on the basis of birthplace. They want stones to compete on looks alone. Actually, they do in every sector of the market but that of fine goods. But with treatment so pervasive and, in many cases, destructive to internal signs of origin, defending the tradition of origin-selling for ruby may be impossible—unless new origin authentication tests are devised.

CALLING THE SHOTS

As heating has become an indispensable step in the market preparation of ruby, the Thais have come to exert a control of the ruby market which resembles that of De Beers in the diamond world. Like De Beers,

THAI RUBY

the Thais are involved in every aspect of marketing—from mining through cutting and heating. But whereas De Beers can be called a cartel (or, if you prefer, cooperative), the Thai dealer clique that controls the ruby market should be called an oligarchy. Its power is looser and less formal than De Beers'—but often just as awesome.

Just ask the U.S. dealers who have had to contend with it.

Since the dollar started its descent in September 1985, Thai dealers have raised prices for all sizes and grades of ruby, on average, 30% to 50% per year to offset—some say over-compensate for—the greenback's steady loss in value against the Japanese yen, Swiss franc and deutsche mark. And as long as the Japanese, Chinese and Koreans who are the current big buyers of ruby make no protest, the Thais will show no mercy at the bargaining table. So U.S. dealers are forced to pass up nearly all the ruby offered them. The Thais are inflexible, willing only to haggle at most a few percentage points about price. As a result, American dealers set on buying goods have been returning home empty-handed. There's really not much else they can do on the buying end.

Ironically, some Americans are taking advantage of runaway prices in Bangkok by selling ruby stocks in Thailand for 20% to 30% more than they would receive in New York. It's either that or wait until domestic buyers are willing to pay what everyone else is paying. So far, U.S. jewelry manufacturers and retailers have been balking at higher ruby prices and, instead, concentrating on emerald and sapphire. Eventually, suppliers are hoping, customers will re-commence ruby buying with their old ferocity. "It's just a matter of convincing the industry that high ruby prices in Bangkok are here to stay," says a dealer. Judging from jeweler resistance so far, it might be better to hope that the U.S. dollar regains some of its old clout as a currency. Meanwhile the high cost of ruby has put this gem off limits to most American jewelers.

EAST AFRICAN FANCY SAPPHIRE

Twenty-two miles from the Indian Ocean, at a small bend in Tanzania's Umba River near the Kenyan border, you'll find a unique two-mile-radius corundum pipe that produces just about every color of sapphire imaginable. Since the pipe's discovery in 1962, its distinctive stones have earned the name Umba sapphire.

Around 1965, a family of gem dealers cornered the Tanzanian fancy sapphire market by jointly buying most of Umba's output. Nearly 25 years later, more than half the rough the family bought—said to be the lion's share of Umba's production—is still uncut and the corner is still theirs.

That there is far more unfinished than finished Umba fancy color sapphire indicates that accceptance of African corundum lags far behind that from Asia, principally Sri Lanka and Burma. Although the Japanese began to take a keen interest in pink sapphire during the late 1980s, their taste ran to saturate pure pink colors that Africa does not produce—or, at least, hasn't so far.

Evidently, however, there are those who think that somewhere in the pipe at Umba lie pinks that will excite buyers as much as those from Asia. And they are willing to spend the big bucks needed to put their hunch to the test. When sapphire mining at Umba was merely a pick-and-shovel affair, it was far less expensive and risky to find out what was there. By the time the pipe had been worked to a depth of 100 feet, costly underground shaft mining became necessary. But given the political climate in Africa, few companies wanted to make the investment this kind of mining requires.

Tanzania is a socialist country whose mercurial leaders ordered sapphire mining at Umba shut down in 1970. Fearful of more expulsions, mining companies stayed away. Then, when the government permitted far freer enterprise in 1987, a Japanese consortium worked out a deal with the state to start heavy mining. The agreement took the gem world by surprise because it had been assumed that powerful Chinese gem trade interests in either Hong Kong or Thailand would be the highest bidders for the rights to work the Umba pipe.

Will the enormous expenditure pay off? Dealers worldwide are waiting to find out—but not exactly with bated breath. Umba sapphires per se have still to find a wide following. So if the new production isn't significantly better than the old, the market just faces more of an overhang.

Of course, it's always possible that attitudes toward Umba sapphire will change markedly in the next few years. Dealers who specialize in African gems say that jewelry makers and retailers are slowly beginning

EAST AFRICAN FANCY SAPPHIRE

to recognize Umba sapphire on its own terms. What's more, African fancy color sapphire has benefited from a new openness to fancy color sapphire in general since the early 1980s, especially stones in the pink family. While Umba is not known for rose pinks, it excels (or, at least, excelled) in pinkish-orange shades (variously described as "salmon" to "peach" colors) that have begun to catch the public's eye. As important, Umba has given the world sapphires with unique hues and color changes that are found nowhere else. What follows is a quick glimpse of East Africa's sapphire spectrum.

PADPARADSCHA—OR WORD PLAY?
Without a doubt, the most famous (some say infamous) Tanzanian fancy sapphires are its so-called "padparadschas." When the firm with a corner on Umba's production began cutting and selling East African orange sapphires in the mid-1960s, it used this somewhat provocative designation. Purists who believe that padparadschas proper hail only from Sri Lanka (Ceylon) objected so much that the firm now calls its stones "African padparadschas."

Why do so many in the trade insist on this differentiation? One West Coast dealer explains that most African padparadschas have a strong tinge of brown that is noticeably absent from the Asian variety. Nevertheless, this dealer maintains that some East African padparadschas have an indisputable right to be sold as such—regardless of origin. An importer in Cost Mesa, Calif., agrees that there are East African padparadschas, but still sells such stones as "fancy pink-orange sapphires" only. "The trade doesn't seem ready to accept the notion that bona fide padparadschas can come from Africa," he says. Whether called "padparadscha" or not, many of these stones, even ones with some brown, have deep distinctive burnt orange and salmon colors that merit some attention from consumers.

HAUNTING DEEP PURPLES
East African sapphire has no peer in the purple range. The most superb of these stones have what one Bermuda dealer describes as an "intense cherry-orchid purple."

ALEXANDRITE-LIKE SAPPHIRES
Much pink and purple fancy sapphire (as well as garnet) from East Africa changes colors in diverse ways when taken from daylight to incandescent light. The predominant color change resembles that of alexandrite.

EAST AFRICAN FANCY SAPPHIRE

Stones that look greenish to grayish blue in daylight turn a pronounced violet to cranberry red in incandescent light. Already these color-change sapphires have become a hot collector's item. But dealers hope for an even brighter future for them with that small but determined segment of the public that wants, but cannot find or afford, fine alexandrite.

CANARIES, GOLDS AND YELLOWS
Admirers of East African fancy sapphire, of whom there are suddenly quite a few, think Umba's yellow and golden hues more than hold their own in side-by-side comparisons with their Asian counterparts. To give comparable depth of color, most yellow sapphires from Sri Lanka must first be heated. But East African stones are so rich and full that they do not need color coaxing in the oven. What's more, they are a bargain.

IN—AND OUT—OF THE PINK
When it comes to pink, East African fancy sapphire does not seem to compare favorably with Asian goods. First of all, African production is dwarfed by that from Sri Lanka. Next, East African pinks tend to be overloaded with silk which tends to make them look overly sleepy. Possibly heat treatment could reduce this silk, but one of the strong points for East African sapphire has been its "all-natural" status. Some dealers feel that heating would put them in too much of a bind regarding disclosure as far as selling goes. Besides, many stones boast a secondary brown which heating may not remove anyway.

RAINBOWS ON THE WRIST
East Africa has produced large numbers of small-sized pastel-color fancy sapphires. Individually, most of these stones are too pale for jewelry use. But when combined, they have definite appeal. In fact, dealers have been assembling these pastel-color East African sapphires into inexpensive all-corundum "rainbow" assortments suitable for bracelets and necklaces. Dealers report strong sales of rainbow suites in round and square shapes between 2 and 4mm.

KASHMIR SAPPHIRE

You hear so much about the hands-down superiority of the Kashmir sapphire over every other variety of this blue corundum that sooner or later you feel obligated to put this trade dictum to a test. So I arranged for a private showing of Kashmir sapphires at the office of a connoisseur gem specialist.

It only takes one stone, the very first one I see, to make a believer of me. The stone's blue is rich, royal and velvety, the quintessence of sapphire color. And because the gem is 24 carats, the telltale color banding that supposedly confirms Kashmir origin is immediately noticeable. Beyond such brief details, the mouth- and eye-watering beauty of this sapphire is hard to convey.

Astonishingly, this magnificent gem, which has papers tracing it back at least 75 years, probably sold for less than $1 per carat when it was still in its rough state. Today, the finished masterpiece could fetch as much as $60,000 per carat, close to $1.5 million, in a posh Fifth Avenue or Rodeo Drive jewelry salon.

But if $60,000 per carat strikes you as too steep a price for a sapphire, even one so pedigreed, another Kashmir stone we examined, this one only 6 carats, can be bought for $45,000 per carat. Smaller size and a slightly lighter tone prevent it from commanding as much as the 24-carat splendor. Yet this stone, which its owner casually dismisses as "fine but not gem," is better than most sapphires jewelers and dealers may ever see. Once again, the color is a serenely soft, almost princely blue with the same giveaway color banding. When put next to a fabulous 8-carat Sri Lankan sapphire, the latter seems sharper, cooler, less sensuous (although still gorgeous).

So much for the ineffable beauty of Kashmir sapphire. Rarely, except in a few tanzanites, has this writer seen a blue that was as awe-inspiring. And yet, these Kashmir sapphires may fall far short of the standard this species set after it first flooded the gem market late in the last century.

BLASÉ ABUNDANCE

Believe it or not, when sapphires were discovered around 1882 in Kashmir, a small Indian state in the northwest Himalayas, they were so plentiful and large that locals would pick them off the ground to use as flint stones. When they realized these rocks were facetable, they took them to Indian dealers in places like Delhi who bought them as amethysts for pennies a carat. Later, when the gems were properly identified as corundum, their prices jumped. Gemologist Max Bauer reports in the 1904 edition of "The Systematic Description of Precious Stones" that

KASHMIR SAPPHIRE

the usual price for Kashmir sapphire rough in London, then a major colored stone cutting center, was 20 pounds (or $120) per ounce (86 cents per carat). However, the price fell when the market was glutted with this material.

Who could have foreseen that the Kashmir deposits would be nearly depleted by 1925? Even after the mines were nearly exhausted, dealers learning their craft in London in the 1930s recollect that prices never exceeded $500 per carat. Despite the sharp decline in production, sporadic parcels still made their way to the West. Even today, smugglers continue to bring out occasional stones, despite heavy police guarding of the known mine sites. No official sales of Kashmir rough have taken place in nearly 20 years—although it was announced in 1988 that mining would re-commence. Meanwhile, the reputation of Kashmir sapphire endures so strongly that fine stones from this region are entitled to breathtaking premiums—based, in large part, on origin. The trouble is that proving origin is nowadays exceedingly tricky.

PROVENANCE PROBLEMS

No matter what dealers say, selling a sapphire as Kashmir is usually more a matter of faith than fact. Indeed, many gems sold as Kashmir later turn out to be heated Sri Lankan stand-ins whose oven-induced color zoning was mistaken for the banding associated with the Himalayan variety.

For this reason, buying stones reputed to be Kashmir often involves what one New York gem dealer describes as "agonizing judgment calls." Sometimes these calls have little or nothing to do with the stones and everything to do with the seller. "My decision is based as much on who shows me the stone and how as the stone itself," he continues. "If the person showing it is just back from the Far East with a paper full of sapphires, he's already got two strikes against him."

Even when this dealer is shown blue-ribbon laboratory reports that vouch for the stone's Kashmir origin, he is not impressed. "The finest labs have been dead wrong," he says. Far more important to him, as far as papers go, is documentation of previous ownership that can help him trace back the stone enough years to make him feel secure about its origin. The trade calls such documentation "provenance" and is becoming increasingly dependent on it, much the same way the fine arts world has long been. Many of the dealer's finest stones have extensive background papers.

Still, proving origin or, at least, becoming secure enough about it to

KASHMIR SAPPHIRE

begin negotiating for a stone on the basis of it, is only the first step in acquiring a Kashmir sapphire, says one gem importer. "There always comes a time for a one-on-one confrontation with the gem," he says. "This is the moment when you give the stone a ruthless examination. That means forgetting everything you have ever heard about it and deciding for yourself what the stone is and if you like it. Just being a Kashmir sapphire is no guarantee of beauty or value."

Such a confrontation takes know-how and is not recommended for anyone who only buys fine sapphires occasionally. Indeed, such a buyer may be better off ignoring origin, unless the person from whom he buys a Kashmir stone has impeccable credentials with such material and will attest to origin in writing. One sapphire specialist does just that and, by so doing, accepts full liability should the stone turn out otherwise than claimed.

Given the extreme difficulty of verifying Kashmir origin these days, many in the trade think origin selling is a dangerous anachronism that should be done away with. Instead, they favor judging a gem's beauty and merit in terms of universal color grading systems. Advocates of this approach say that laboratory grades will reflect the inherent superiority of Kashmir color, thus protecting these stones' values and, at the same time, eliminating the need to sell them on the basis of locality.

One New York appraiser says sacrificing origin and background and reducing a gem to a lab grade takes the all-important elements of "heritage and history" out of gem ownership. According to him, that's a no-no for Kashmir sapphire, a gem that has a stature with connoisseurs that can be likened to that of a Rubens painting in the art world. Validation has become as difficult—and as necessary—for the gem masterpiece as for the art masterpiece. "Just because authentication work is hard is no reason to take the easy way out and abandon it," this appraiser warns. "You let grading take precedence over everything else and pretty soon the colored stone world is going to be as sterile as the diamond world."

PADPARADSCHA SAPPHIRE

It is almost a macho obligation these days for precious stone dealers to say they are versed in padparadscha sapphire, the rarest and most prized fancy corundum in the world.

Yet one New York lapidary, an acknowledged expert on the species, says that after nearly 25 years' experience buying padparadschas, he has seen fewer than 10 that qualify as fine specimens of this stone.

" 'Padparadscha' is one of the most abused gem names I can think of," he says. "In fact, Ceylonese dealers use it as a catch-all term for any sapphire that can't be considered ruby."

Given the paucity of true padparadschas, it is easy to understand why there is so much confusion in the trade about this gem. The confusion has widened in recent years as fancy sapphires in general have zoomed in popularity. And it will grow worse if more dealers seek acceptance for use of the term "padparadscha" in conjunction with marketing a certain kind of East African fancy sapphire. Already some West Coast dealers claim that a select few of these African stones are indistinguishable from their Asian counterparts.

That's news to the East Coast.

"I have yet to see an African fancy sapphire that could be called padparadscha," says one New York cutter. "I'm anxious to see one."

Meanwhile an important question remains: Just what is padparadscha?

The answer has much to do with what it's not. This process of elimination helps to narrow sharply the number of candidates for the padparadscha category and thus reduces confusion. But be warned at the outset: Padparadscha is a gem that requires great savvy to buy. Those who lack it need a trustworthy jeweler with good credentials in the fancy sapphire area.

FROM SANSKRIT TO SLANG
The trade can be partially excused for its liberality with the padparadscha label. In the last 100 or so years, the term has undergone several important refinements in meaning. These are detailed in a superb article on padparadscha by gemologist Robert Crowningshield published in the spring 1983 issue of *Gems and Gemology,* the journal of the Gemological Institute of America.

Apparently, the term "padparadscha" is derived from an ancient Sanskrit word *(padmaraga)* for the lotus flower and its color. From there it makes its way into Sinalhese *(padmaragaya)* and ultimately into German *(padparaschan)*. When it finally surfaces as a term applied to gems

PADPARADSCHA SAPPHIRE

(Crowningshield dates its earliest usage as such to 1849), it carries a seemingly different color connotation than it does now.

A century ago, the word we know today as padparadscha referred to a ruby sub-grouping and was used to describe a pinkish-red corundum. By the time Max Bauer, whom Crowningshield calls "the dean of gemological writers," pronounces on the gem in 1909, it has become a "reddish-yellow" fancy sapphire. In 1932, Bauer gives the gem its modern spelling and modifies his description to "orange to reddish yellow." Today, of course, the term is more specifically associated with a pinkish-orange (some say orangy-pink) fancy sapphire. The colors red and yellow are rarely, if ever, mentioned at all.

The term "padparadscha" has not only been restricted in terms of color scope but also in terms of tone and origin. Tone, as Crowningshield says, "should be limited to light to medium" ones. Origin, of course, is strictly Ceylonese (Sri Lankan).

However, just because the term "padparadscha" seems to have changed meaning over the years, it is doubtful that the centuries-old aesthetic ideal for this stone has. Indeed, one cutter believes that these changes really represent "a pinpointing of meaning" so that the term more nearly mirrors the mental image that experts have of padparadscha. In this way, the term lends itself much less to abuse. "There was always a very narrow margin of acceptable color for padparadscha," he says.

OF SALMON AND SUNSETS

Because the jewelry industry has not yet adopted any standardized color measurement system, there is no way to precisely quantify the amount of orange and pink, plus their combined tonal strength, that constitutes padparadscha color. Lacking such measurements, dealers must resort to metaphor in order to describe the proper mixture of hues.

For instance, according to a West Coast importer, the term padparadscha conjures up images of "luscious lox (salmon) slices." These metaphoric descriptions eliminate from consideration many of the reddish-orange and brownish-orange fancy sapphires that often pass for padparadscha.

In general, true padparadschas must have the distinctive but delicate pinkish-orange sunset/salmon color in just the right balance and intensity. To get that color, jewelers will probably have to look for stones in excess of 5 carats. "Padparadscha needs a certain amount of body mass to get its full color going," says a New York padparadscha expert. "Most of the fine stones I've seen are at least 5 and often 10 carats or more."

PADPARADSCHA SAPPHIRE

In addition, he notes, stones will have to be fairly clean. Visible inclusions can dull and flatten even the finest padparadscha color. Dealers want vitality as much as proper hue.

All of this translates into the kind of prices for a clean, well-cut, true-color Ceylonese padparadscha that one might expect to pay for a pedigreed Kashmir sapphire—which means big bucks. What are called "African padparadschas" will cost far less for top stones.

"The so-called 'African padparadschas' from the Umba River region of Tanzania have far more brown and orange than true Ceylonese padparadschas," says a West Coast expert on African stones. "Although they are as beautiful as fancy sapphires, they lack the delicate balance of pink and orange that means so much in padparadscha."

Nevertheless, there seems to be growing jeweler acceptance of certain African fancy sapphires as padparadschas. Indeed, we visited a carriage trade store in Philadelphia whose proprietor, a savvy gem buyer, proudly showed us a dark brownish-pink-orange sapphire from Umba when we asked to see a padparadscha. When we dismissed the stone as an African fancy sapphire and not a true padparadscha, the jeweler insisted we were wrong. A few years back, the same jeweler would never have allowed an African fancy sapphire to substitute for a true Sri Lankan padparadscha.

Maybe we're being too prissy, but we think jewelers should stick with traditional definitions of this rare sapphire's color. As one dealer puts it: "Fine padparadscha is far rarer than either fine Kashmir sapphire or Burma ruby. We're talking about a true Rembrandt among gemstones."

PINK SAPPHIRE

When one gem importer buys pink sapphire from Burma tribesmen, they call it ruby—and don't take kindly to contradiction.

When another importer buys pink sapphire from Sri Lankan dealers, they call it padparadscha (an extremely rare pinkish-orange sapphire)—and act offended if you suggest otherwise.

For hundreds of years, Asian dealers have been calling pink sapphire all kinds of things.

Everything but what it is.

Until recently, many gem dealers in America took after them—insisting pink sapphire was, at the very least, pale ruby. As a result, pink sapphire had to fight an uphill battle to be recognized in its own right. Now the stone is finally beginning to have a wide following as a fancy sapphire, and does not have to pretend to be something it isn't.

"America is waking up to the fact that there is sapphire that isn't blue," says a New York lapidary. "It may sound crazy, but there was a time when jewelers didn't know or recognize any other color in a sapphire."

Given such color blindness, dealers with inventories of pink fancy sapphire who wished to be honest about their goods had to sit on them—unless they had deep reddish-pink stones from Burma that many in the trade considered ruby. Even today, these Burmese fancy sapphires are the center of a raging nomenclature controversy regarding the crossover point from pink sapphire to ruby. Many dealers, as well as gemologists, contend that calling any pink corundum "sapphire" is a misnomer. Pink, they argue, is simply light red and, therefore, all such stones should be called ruby. If the trade must use the term pink, this faction urges that such stones be known as pink ruby rather than pink sapphire.

But pink sapphire specialists seem content to leave things as they are. "It's a gemological issue. Pink is just different than red," says one New York gem dealer. "So leave the pink corundums associated with sapphire and the red ones associated with ruby." It is a sign of pink sapphire's growing acceptance that more and more dealers agree with him.

THINKING PINK

The sapphire-versus-ruby nomenclature battle revolves around money. Since ruby is usually far more expensive than sapphire, it is hoped that being able to call sapphire ruby will entitle dealers to charge more for it. That's hoping for a lot. A name change could help at most in a handful of cases, ones involving reddish-pink Burmese sapphires that might qualify as borderline rubies. But the rest of the time, calling pink red makes about as much sense as calling black white.

PINK SAPPHIRE

Quite frankly, one doubts whether the nomenclature battle is worth waging over the vast majority of pink sapphires, most of them from Sri Lanka and far lighter than the exceptionally rare Burmese stones that many swear are rubies. Anyone who has seen parcels of standard Sri Lankan pink sapphire knows that labeling these stones as "ruby" is stretching the term rather thin.

That doesn't stop people from trying, especially dealers and gemologists armed with a smattering of color science. They'll tell you pink isn't even a recognized spectrum color, merely "de-saturated red." Maybe so, but pink is, and has always been, recognized as a color distinct from red in the jewelry and, for that matter, fashion worlds. In fact, even dealers who long ago insisted that pink sapphire was the same as ruby implicitly acknowledged there is a difference between pink and red stones by dividing ruby into two categories: "feminine" for pink and "masculine" for red.

Today, pink sapphire needs no favors or apologies. On the contrary, the recent popularity of pastel-color gems has opened doors for pink sapphire and given it Cadillac status among the many gem varieties being used to meet the demand for pink. Since early 1987 alone, prices for robustly pink sapphires have jumped 30% to 40% annually, mainly the result of discovery by pay-any-price Japanese connoisseurs. Nevertheless, the best of the breed in a 3-carat size still only command roughly one-half the price of their 3-carat superfine Thai ruby counterparts.

"Best of the breed" in pink sapphire is often described as "hot pink," a pure, vibrant color with no violet or purple. It is assumed such stones are from Burma, a major gem source which has been closed to the outside world since 1962, resulting in a dearth of these stones. That leaves Sri Lanka, the prime source for pink sapphire, to occasionally provide highly saturate pink stones on a par with those from Burma—but not often enough to challenge Burma's preeminence in this gem.

Even so, Sri Lanka produces many pretty pinks. For the most part, they tend to be light and lively, usually with highly visible amounts of violet and purple. Generally, explains one dealer, the more violet the stone, the lower its price. Strongly violet stones in 1- to 3-carat sizes present the biggest bargains for consumers. Punchier, pinker stones in the same size range can run three to four times more while a pure pink color can add still 50% more to the price. For exceedingly scarce stones above 5 carats, price reflects the fact that this is a seller's—not a buyer's—market.

PINK SAPPHIRE

BUYING TIPS

As we said before, pink sapphires which command top dollar are from Burma, or, should we say, assumed to be from Burma. Some dealers who aren't sure of or don't wish to be pinned down on country of origin will describe stones as "Burma-like" or "as good as Burma." But the point is this: Burma means top-grade.

Whether or not an exemplary pink sapphire is actually from Burma, such stones always have two traits that go hand in hand: intensity and tone that push the stone beyond any association with pastel color.

But color alone does not justify premium prices for pink sapphire. While not as important as color, clarity has a big bearing on the value of pink sapphire. Indeed, one drawback of Burma stones, comments a New York gem dealer who specializes in connoisseur stones, is their tendency to be more included than the Sri Lankan variety. Because most pink sapphire is lighter in tone and less saturate in color than ruby, dealers advise jewelers to buy eye-clean stones. "Inclusions are much more noticeable in pastel-color stones," notes another dealer.

While on the subject of quality factors in pink sapphire, we must cite brilliance. Although partly a function of clarity, brilliance is affected by cutting and polishing, too. Dealers say that many pink sapphires cut in Sri Lanka are so badly botched that they are deprived of the brilliance they could have. Thankfully, most feel they can turn to Thailand, which in the last decade has emerged as the world's major sapphire cutting center for fine cuts.

But a handful of perfectionists aren't even satisfied with the work of Thailand's cutters. Instead, they reserve the finishing touches for themselves. "The best cutting of sapphire is still done in the United States and Europe," one of them insists.

SRI LANKAN SAPPHIRE

One by one, the world's most renowned deposits of blue sapphire are running dry or simply not running at all.

Kashmir, the supreme source for less than 50 years, has been a lost cause since the 1920s when production all but petered out. More recently, in 1962, Burma sealed off its fabled Mogok tract, leaving the world dependent ever since on intrepid smugglers for the greatly diminished supply of her coveted corundums. In 1974, Cambodia's famed Paillin region was decreed, and has remained, off-limits to gem mining. And about 10 years ago, Thailand's Katchanaburi sapphire fields ceased to be worth the time and trouble to work.

All this, says one New York dealer, has left Sri Lanka (still stubbornly called Ceylon by old timers) "the only steady producer left of large fine sapphire." Now some may argue that Montana's sapphire-rich Yogo Gulch could re-emerge as a reliable source, too. But so far, chronic financial woes that have plagued every recent attempt at mining there have left it more a source of big hopes than big stones. No such hopes are entertained for Australia, the world's chief source of low-end blue sapphire, or newcomer East Africa.

So when it comes to newly mined fine blue sapphire, Sri Lanka is now the standard bearer for this species. Her status as the world's prime producer of fine blue sapphire comes at a time when Sri Lanka continues to grow as a sapphire mining center. One Sri Lankan dealer reports that several finds have been made recently in the southern part of his country. "The goods are there," he says. But he quickly notes, "Fine sapphires are the scarcest they've been in decades."

The reasons, he believes, have more to do with man than nature. A fierce battle for control of the Sri Lankan sapphire market is driving prices for goods to dizzying heights. And the strong comeback of the fine goods market during the dollar's long post-1985 decline only accelerated this trend.

FROM BLAH TO BLUE

Sri Lankan sapphire, like Brazilian aquamarine, is a stone that is customarily heated to permanently improve color. Indeed, low-temperature, charcoal-fire heat has been used for centuries in Sri Lanka to sharpen hue and spruce up appearance. But this method has limited application. It didn't do much good for the vast number of the country's milky, rutile-ridden stones.

In the mid-1970s, gem dealers in Thailand began to experiment with high-heat kilns and later controlled-atmosphere furnaces to transform

SRI LANKAN SAPPHIRE

once seemingly heat-resistant sapphires from colorless to color-fast corundums. Heating turned cloudy stones clear and induced deep blue colors. To experienced eyes, these heated stones were distinguishable by their pronounced color zoning, altered inclusions and, on occasion, their "scorched" color.

"The impact of the new heating technology was felt far more in the commercial than the fine goods sector," says a New York cutter. "There was suddenly an enormous influx of pleasing lower and middle cost Sri Lankan sapphire."

The influx couldn't have come at a better time. As 1970s inflation drove up sapphire prices and Far East Asian political turbulence disrupted fresh supplies, Sri Lanka's heatable sapphires became a godsend. By 1980, word was out that Thai dealers had found a way, one some gemologists contend was borrowed from American crystal growers, to coax color out of what formerly had been considered incorrigible corundums.

Now known as "Geuda" stones, these remedial roughs began to command higher and higher prices. Thai dealers, jealous guardians of the new high-heat color technology, were willing to pay those prices. Sri Lankan dealers watched helplessly while Bangkok replaced Colombo as the world's corundum capital—at least for commercial material. "To become the true leader," says a New York fine gems expert, "Thailand must offer the complete range of sapphire from top to bottom."

Evidently, the Thais are succeeding in doing just that.

ALL NATURAL OR NOTHING

In the last few years, Thai dealers have been making a bid to dominate in fine sapphire as well as intermediate and lower grades. One way they are positioning themselves as fine sapphire specialists, equal to Sri Lanka's best, is to discreetly comb the American market for sapphires. Often working through European and American proxies, the Thais have taken advantage of laggard prices in the U.S. fine goods market—due entirely to the dollar's slide. There they can pick up stones for 20% to 25% less than they can be sold for in Bangkok and as much as 40% below their price in Colombo.

The bargains exist because U.S. jewelry manufacturers and retailers balked at upward cost adjustments for sapphire as the dollar lost purchasing power against the Japanese yen, Swiss franc and German mark.

But while the U.S. fine sapphire market holds its breath, the international market pants for goods. Significantly, many buyers of fine, large

SRI LANKAN SAPPHIRE

sapphires are demanding that stones be unheated—and documented as such. Cap Beesley of American Gemological Laboratories in New York, the most highly respected lab for treatment documentation in America other than the Gemological Institute of America (GIA), says, "More and more buyers are making purchase of fine sapphires and rubies conditional upon inspection of stones for treatment and clearance of them as natural." By "clearance," Beesley doesn't just mean issuing a certificate that is free of any damning heat-treatment comments. Such certificates leave room for errors of omission. Therefore, Beesley continues, "Buyers want to see an explicit positive comment that the stone is straight."

Accordingly, consumers should expect to pay anywhere from 30% to 50% more for a fine Sri Lankan sapphire from 3 to 10 carats that is certified uncooked by either AGL or GIA. In the case of sapphires of 10 carats or more, the premium for untreated stones starts at 50% and moves higher, depending on size and beauty.

Such premiums could widen considerably and a full-fledged two-tier market emerge for unheated as opposed to heated sapphire as the public becomes more aware of treatment. This is more likely than ever before now that the American Gem Trade Association, a leading U.S. gem dealer group, has prepared a disclosure system, endorsed by retailer groups like Jewelers of America and the American Gem Society, to inform consumers about this sensitive subject.

STAR SAPPHIRE

Blessed is the corundum that contains rutile. Not only does this mineral produce asterism—the star-effect—in sapphires, it also acts as a bluing agent when combined with iron. There's only one drawback.

Rutile (titanium oxide) can't perform both feats at once. It has to be in different chemical states to make stars and to make color. If left in its undissolved state where it clusters in dense bundles of microscopic needles, abundant rutile causes corundums to become anything from translucent to opaque. Usually corundums with heavy concentrations of rutile have a milky appearance, which is why it is called "silk" in the trade. Fortunately, stones with partially dissolved rutile have redeeming gray and light-to-medium blue colors. When cut into cabochons, these stones frequently reflect light along their domes in a six-rayed star pattern—the result of corundum's six-sided crystal structure.

Cabbing into star stones was the fate of many rutile-rich—otherwise useless—corundums for centuries. Then about 15 years ago, dealers in Bangkok, out to make Thailand the world's No.1 sapphire cutting center, discovered the effects of dissolving rutile in ovens. Altered-state rutile turned cloudy stones clear and bland stones blue—permanently.

This alchemical breakthrough sent Bangkok cutters scurrying to Sri Lanka to buy up heat-transformable stones by the ton from dealers ignorant of their latent beauty and glad to be rid of them at pennies per carat. By the time Sri Lanka's gem trade caught on to the Thais' corundum capers, these tiny silk purses disguised as sow's ears were known as "Geuda" goods and far from cheap. As Sri Lanka's mountainous backlogs of Geuda material became molehills, the Thais began to heat many Geudas that had been already cut into star sapphires, hoping the rutile in these stones would work the same color and clarity magic. When they found it did, the hunt was on for treatment-worthy stars.

Consequently, star sapphire has become the first major casualty of modern gem enhancement as large numbers of potential and existing star stones are earmarked for oven burning in Bangkok. But long before Thai cooking endangered this gem species, star sapphire suffered a foretaste of high-tech trauma with the introduction of a U.S.-made synthetic variety.

THE LINDE YEARS

As good as nature is at producing stars in sapphires, she is no match for man. That became obvious when Union Carbide debuted the first synthetic star sapphires, trademarked as Linde Stars, in the late 1940s. The new manmades boasted stars with sharp, straight rays that made

STAR SAPPHIRE

most of the natural variety's best seem crooked and blurry by comparison. No matter that the perfection of the Linde star offended, and still offends, traditionalists. Consumers took to the synthetics' straight-legged star, so much so that four decades later they have come to expect rays in the far more expensive natural variety that walk lines as straight and narrow as those made in the laboratory.

That's asking a lot of natural star sapphires, especially those with the medium-intensity blue color connoisseurs associate with this species. As said before, asterism results when light reflects from large clusters of rutile needles most common to the corundum found in Sri Lanka. The more densely packed and fine those needles, the more pronounced and precise the star.

Union Carbide and the present major practitioner of its star sapphire manufacturing process, Nakazumi Earth Crystals in Japan, cram rutile fibers far smaller than those found in natural stones together to make a star so vivid and intense it looks, in the words of Gemological Institute of America chief gemologist John Koivula, "painted on the stone rather than emanating from within it. That's why these almost branded-in stars are considered a tip-off to laboratory origin."

But despite stars that lack depth and often appear like decals, synthetic stones have clearly put dealers on the defensive—a tribute to the crystal grower's art. While showing us stones for this story, expert after expert felt the need to apologize for the diffuse, uneven, sometimes stubby rays of the natural variety, especially common with deep-blue colors.

THE CURSE OF FINE CUTTING

Apologies don't do much good, however. Since star sapphire is first and foremost a phenomenon stone, the quality of the star logically means more to jewelers and consumers than color. Hence it is hardly surprising that star sapphire specialists report selling three times as many top grays as top blues. The stars in gray stones are generally better—meaning each ray fully extends to the base of the cabochon.

Fine stars aren't all that gray stones have going for them. Usually, they benefit from superior make. Because blue stones tend to be more translucent than gray ones, cutters have to keep much more of the original rough (and, with it, rutile) to retain intensity of asterism and color. Therefore, blue stars are generally cut with sagging bellies while grays are cut with flat ones. Jewelers and consumers who do not understand that big bottoms help preserve stars and color resent what they think is needless extra weight and expense.

STAR SAPPHIRE

The ubiquity of slim, trim Lindes and nice-make natural grays only makes it harder for dealers to explain why so many deep-blue star sapphires are overweight. Forgetting for a minute that unsightly bottom bulk can be hidden in mountings, the deep-blue star sapphire with near-perfect asterism offers consumers one mighty consolation for excess underneath: rarity.

Yet even with one or two legs missing sections, fine blue stones can command hefty per-carat prices in 10-carat sizes. And if all the legs are distinct and intact, the per-carat price of stones can double—that is, if you can find any. Prices ease a bit for fine blues in 5-carat sizes, the minimum size dealers recommend for this species to look its best.

Nevertheless, the somewhat steep prices of fine blues make far less expensive gray and powder-blue colors very palatable to most jewelers and their customers. At per-carat prices as little as $\frac{1}{10}$ those of topcolor blues with good, well-centered stars, who can blame them? For a little extra money, consumers might consider stones with a powder blue color.

But whatever color you choose, don't delay your purchase for too long. Prices will almost surely rise if the dollar resumes any kind of sharp slide against the Japanese yen. As one New York star sapphire specialist points out, "The Japanese are big buyers of phenomenon stones. So whenever the yen strengthens against the dollar, it gives them more of a buying advantage in Thailand and other Far East sapphire cutting centers."

YELLOW SAPPHIRE

Before 1980, sapphire was synonymous with blue. Few jewelers cared that the gem came in other colors—including yellow and gold.

They weren't alone. Most sapphire dealers showed the same indifference to non-blue sapphires.

One of the few exceptions is a New York lapidary who remembers buying the finest yellows and goldens for next to nothing on his frequent trips to the Far East during the early 1960s. "Dealers in Ceylon [Sri Lanka—then and now the world's chief mining center for fine sapphire] didn't even want to be bothered with fancy color sapphires—certainly not yellow," he recalls. "They stored the rough in big sacks and cut it on days when there was nothing else to do if you wanted to keep busy."

All that's changed. Sri Lankan dealers make a point of showing him their best fancy yellow sapphires. The situation is the same in Thailand, the world's central market for polished sapphire. A New York specialist in premium jewelry reports seeing almost as much yellow as blue sapphire on a recent buying trip to Bangkok. "There were so many yellow sapphires that I was stunned," he says.

What is behind this decade's supply-side explosion of yellow and golden sapphire? The same thing that's behind the supply-side explosion of better-color ruby and blue sapphire in the preceding decade: heat treatment.

Today Thailand is to corundum heat treatment what Silicon Valley is to computers. Although this form of gemstone color enhancement has been used for centuries, the Thais have taken it to new and as yet unmatched levels of sophistication over the past 15 years.

This technological edge has allowed dealers in that Southeast Asian country to just about corner the corundum market. The Thais can offer gem miners in far-flung places like Australia, Sri Lanka and Kenya prices none of their competitors dare to because heating will permanently improve enough stones (e.g., by de-clouding milky sapphires or removing purple from rubies) to justify paying more.

If it weren't for oven alchemy, it is doubtful that there would be adequate supplies of ruby and conventional sapphire to meet skyrocketing world demand. In the case of yellow sapphire, however, the surge in supply has not been equalled by a surge in demand. Indeed, the endless profusion of heated stones suggests there is production for the sake of production—making this yellow sapphire one of the decade's greatest technological marvels but also one of its greatest marketing mishaps. What went wrong?

YELLOW SAPPHIRE

HIGH HEAT, HIGH HOPES

The rationale for treatment of yellow sapphire is clear. Until very recently, most yellow sapphires that jewelers saw were pale and unattractive. Fine natural yellows and goldens were rare, making these stones of interest mostly to collectors.

But around 1980 some dealers in Thailand, already successful in the salvage of blue sapphire, began experimental heating of pale yellow sapphires. They had nothing to lose because the stones were cheap and plentiful.

The experiments soon paid off. "Wallflower" sapphires were routinely transformed from soft pastel shades to what dealers called "canary" colors—bright, vibrant golden and orangy yellows. How? Heating stones that contained iron at temperatures between 1,600 and 1,900 Centigrade converts the iron to a state where it acts as a strong coloring agent. If chromium is present with the iron, the chemical reaction to heat produces even stronger, more golden colors.

Nevertheless, there was a big difference between the end colors achieved by heating yellow sapphires and those achieved by heating blues. The electric golden hues attained in the oven were rarely, if ever, encountered in nature—while the blues were identical to colors found in the raw. Marketing stones whose colors were, in essence, artificial was a big gamble.

Yet dealers assumed the market would take to enhanced yellow sapphire as readily as enhanced blue sapphire. Anticipating robust demand, they began to speculate on the new material. In no time at all, treated yellow sapphires cost more than untreated ones on the inter-dealer market—even though jeweler and consumer reaction to the oven-colored stones was an unknown.

The new sapphire debuted at the 1982 Tucson Gem Show—an annual trade event which serves as a launching pad and testing ground for every new gem product in the colored stone world. Dealer showcases were congested with heated yellow sapphire. The abundance, it turned out, was a clue to the newcomer's fate. Within months, dealers realized they had a surfeit on their hands and started to cut prices just to unload goods. Eventually, prices nosedived.

Years later, the glut of recognizably treated yellow and golden sapphires hasn't subsided and prices still seek a level where they will trigger demand.

This isn't the case for lighter, natural and natural-appearing stones. These have no trouble selling to jewelers. Ironically, their prices are half

YELLOW SAPPHIRE

those asked for the distinctly treated variety a few years back.

Meanwhile those deep-baked golden-orange stones that were once the talk of the trade are now spurned by dealers. "Some dealers blame the failure of these treated stones to sell on their artificial-looking color," says a New York jewelry appraiser. "Perhaps they should consider that the real culprit may be price. Treatment gives us golden sapphires that fill a color gap and they would sell if made available at prices which reflected a balance of supply and demand."

THE FACTS OF LIFE

Some say the current fall from favor of glaringly heat-treated yellow and golden sapphire is merely part of a cyclical fashion shift from deep to lighter colors. Others contend it is part of a growing disaffection with rampant gemstone tampering.

It's neither. Rather, as the New York appraiser says, "The fall seems to stem from the failure to have tested the market and determined the stone's place in it. Once the stone's market level was found, demand could have been developed on that basis."

Instead, dealers acted as if jewelers and jewelry makers would share their enthusiasm for the new sapphire. They might have if prices for the stones were lower to start with. So expensive were these novelties that some marketers sought to produce lower-cost deep yellow stones by coating oven failures with chemicals, then heating them to create a lovely surface layer of color. This process is called color diffusion. And while it is permanent, it is considered artificial because the color layer is only skin deep. Immersion in solution will reveal that it is a mere coating.

Sellers of color-diffusion sapphires also assumed the market would welcome their stones and were shocked when the trade expressed outrage. The gemological community wasn't any kinder. After a couple of unsavory dealers tried to sneak the color-diffusion stones through its New York Gem Trade Laboratory undetected, the Gemological Institute of America issued "special alert" gemological bulletins to users of its lab. That dashed hopes for these surface-beauty baubles to win acceptance with dealers and, quite possibly, added to the woes of the all-yellow heated variety.

YOGO SAPPHIRE

While buying things American may be in vogue again, national pride hasn't helped sales of sapphires from the country's vast Yogo Gulch deposit in Montana. Sitting in a mid-Manhattan Citibank vault are some 250,000 carats, mostly rough, of blue and violet sapphire, all that remains of possibly the final attempt to make a go of mining at Yogo.

Citibank acquired the goods in satisfaction of a debt owed by publicly traded Intergem Inc., Denver, Colo., the fourth Yogo mining venture since 1956. Intergem closed its Montana sapphire business in 1985 for basically the same reasons as its post-war predecessors: the extremely high cost of mining sapphire in the United States relative to its cost elsewhere. Unlike the alluvial sapphire found in Australia, Sri Lanka and Thailand, Montana's Yogo sapphire is found embedded in hard rock. That makes mining it a very expensive proposition.

To get jewelers to pay the much higher price for Montana's hard-rock sapphire, Intergem embarked on the shrewdest and most daring marketing campaign for Yogo sapphire in its nearly 110-year history. Rather than sell its stones loose, the company launched a line of Yogo jewelry, then tried to capitalize on Montana sapphire's two greatest strengths: its all-American, all-natural (untreated) status.

Those strengths ultimately proved weaknesses. Few jewelers cared about the Yogo sapphire's home-country origin when prices for stones from more widely known localities were so much less. And fewer still cared that Yogo sapphires were the only stones of their kind in the world with a blanket guarantee to be spared heat treatment to improve appearance and color.

Such a no-treatment guarantee was premature, made at a time when gemstone enhancement disclosure was still taboo in the jewelry industry. Thus the guarantee backfired as a marketing tool because it put jewelers in a "Catch-22" dilemma, forcing them to admit most of their other sapphires were treated and thereby inviting a scandal over the concealment of such facts. "The tactic could only have worked if the trade had been disclosing treatment all along," says a gemological consultant. "Since it wasn't, Intergem looked like a bunch of rabble rousers."

CRYING THE BLUES

Raising the sapphire-treatment issue isn't what sunk Intergem, but it didn't help to keep the company afloat either, especially after it spilled the beans about the treatment issue to *The Wall Street Journal* in 1984. Montana sapphire enthusiasts feel the company could have pursued a

YOGO SAPPHIRE

less aggressive positioning policy for the breed than seeking a controversial market niche for it as the world's only untreated sapphire. "Freedom from treatment is a virtue only for very large, fine stones," says one dealer. "But it doesn't matter much with small stones."

Unfortunately, Yogo doesn't produce many large stones. Melee is, and has always been, its forte. That's because the Yogo Gulch deposit, located just about dead center of Montana, is partially the result of igneous (underground volcanic) activity which pushed the lightest, flattest and most buoyant material up to the surface of the find. Although recent geological surveys indicate sapphire reserves at Yogo as deep as 7,000 feet, mining there has never gone much below 250 feet. Hence the small size, flat shape and lighter color of most Montana sapphires that jewelers saw in the past.

Intergem, like preceding Yogo sapphire marketers, hoped that some day deeper mining would yield sufficient numbers of larger, fuller and darker stones to shatter the trade's equation of Montana with pale, shallow-shaped melee. The company never got the chance to prove its hunches. Now it is very likely that no one else will either—at least not for years to come.

The possibility that Citibank's Yogo holdings are, in effect, the Montana mine's last run makes the stones a significant commodity. It also explains why no one at the institution seems in any great hurry to sell the gems—at least not at distress prices. "The Yogo sapphire has enough history to ensure continued interest in it," says the gemological consultant.

A VICTIM OF ITS BEAUTY

Yogo sapphire is as much a victim of its beauty as its past. At their best, the stones have a crisp, violet-blue color that seems almost pastel when compared with the more saturate blues of Burma's, Kashmir's and Sri Lanka's best. For this reason, Yogo beauty doesn't quite fit in with darker contemporary notions of sapphire excellence. The stones had a much easier time of it in the late 19th century, just after they started coming on to the market.

Discovered by gold prospectors in 1879, Yogo Gulch sapphires weren't identified as such until 1885. And serious mining there didn't get underway for nearly 15 years when, around 1900, an English sapphire syndicate began to buy up claims on the mining property. By 1914, this syndicate owned all claims and was in full production. Meanwhile, George Kunz, Tiffany's visionary vice president and tireless advocate

YOGO SAPPHIRE

for American gems, had taken a strong liking to the sapphire. This admiration is reflected in a turn-of-the-century Tiffany catalog which extols Yogo sapphire for unequalled beauty.

World War I practically halted production at the mine. After the war, serious worker and water shortages, double taxation by the U.S. and British governments, and, finally, a devastating cloudburst in 1923, prevented the Yogo mine from reaching its previous output. In 1929, the mine was closed for good and not worked again until 1956.

Since then, at least four venture groups—the last, Intergem Inc., was launched as a $7.2 million limited partnership in 1980—have successfully mined but unsuccessfully marketed Yogo sapphire. All these ventures were unable to overcome deeply ingrained jeweler preconceptions about Montana stones.

As said earlier, Yogo had a reputation for producing mostly flat stones, averaging 10 to 20 points, that were often too much a baby blue to impress jewelers used to overly dark Australian and Thai melee stones. Even vibrant violet-blue stones, such as those we see in Kunz-era Tiffany pieces, jar with modern sapphire color norms.

To its credit, Intergem fought these preconceptions by, one, offering only stones with full pavilions and, two, offering a majority of round brilliants which made more a virtue of the Yogo's light and lively color. In the end, however, price was too big a drawback. Better Yogo melee was 40% to 50% more expensive than its nearest counterpart. And at a time, 1985, when a fine 1-carat Sri Lankan sapphire was lucky to command $2,000 at retail, Intergem was charging almost double for the best of its very few 1-carat stones. Now, with the steady recovery of the sapphire market since 1986, there may be more price parity between Sri Lanka's and Yogo's best.

As for the future of the Yogo deposit, the outlook remains cloudy. On the positive side, geological surveys of the area estimate that as much as 28 million carats, a gradually increasing percentage of it large stones, are left in the ground. Yet the cost of mining, progressively higher at lower depths, almost ensures that Yogo stones will never be competitive. This long-standing fact of life is a bar to further mining. Only unlikely catastrophic sapphire production halts in Asia and Australia might tempt another Montana mining venture soon. Like it or not, hard-rock sapphire mining in America has become synonymous with hard luck.

PINK SPINEL

If there is such a thing as bad karma for gems, pink spinel has it in spades. By rights, this gem should have a far wider following among jewelers. To start with, it is often mistaken for pink sapphire (just as red spinel is for ruby), but costs a lot less—despite greater rarity.

To compound the gem's misfortunes, pink spinel comes from the same highly regarded sources, Burma and Sri Lanka, as pink sapphire. In fact, the two are usually found together in the same gravels.

Although it shares common features and common ground with pink sapphire, pink spinel hasn't shared in the corundum's recent prosperity. At a time when Japanese connoisseurs are so ga-ga over pink sapphire that their buying alone is driving up prices 30% to 40% a year, they pay no attention to pink spinel.

Over in America, where jewelers are just beginning to take notice of pink sapphire, pink spinel suffers a fate even worse than indifference: hostility. Used to thinking of spinel as a cheap jack-of-all-trades birthstone simulant, retailers rarely stock this gem. Here's why:

Long a stalwart among mass-produced synthetics, spinel has been used for years as a stand-in for diamond, aqua and peridot, to name a few. Thus when a dealer oohs and ahs over some intense pink 1-carat natural spinel and asks hundreds of dollars for it, the jeweler who thinks of spinel as a pennies-per-carat manmade is understandably skeptical.

Actually, prices for pink spinel as of late aren't all that high compared to the early 1980s when a small group of investment gem promoters briefly tried to make as hot a market in 1- to 1½-carat red and reddish-pink spinels as the one they had made in rubies of the same size.

After prices for ruby crashed in 1981, those of spinel fell with them—but nowhere near as much. Now you would think that spinel's resiliency relative to ruby would be a plus—but, true to its bad karma, it was a minus. So while prices are generally around 20% to 30% lower today than they were at the market's top, that's still considered much too expensive by most merchants. Only a handful of trade people versed in pink spinel know better.

THE RARITY FACTOR
Spinel in general and pink spinel in particular are relatively rare stones. Jewelers simply assume that natural spinels are as common as the manmade variety. But the abundance of synthetic spinels should not be taken as an indicator of any natural abundance. To the contrary, fine pink spinels are in a class, rarity-wise, with pink topaz—which makes them far scarcer than fine pink sapphires or pink tourmalines.

PINK SPINEL

Maybe too scarce.

In recent years, the trend in colored stone use has been toward cheap, plentiful stones such as amethyst and blue topaz. Now that pink has joined violet and blue as a staple jewelry color, manufacturers are experimenting with gems like rhodolite and pink tourmaline that can be bought in bulk and cut in standard sizes suitable for mass-production items. Pink spinel is too rare and expensive to be considered for high-volume use.

So partisans of pink spinel try to make a case for it as an ideal custom jewelry gem. But it is invariably skipped over for *more* expensive gems such as pink sapphire or pink topaz.

All of this leaves pink spinel in a dilemma: too expensive for the masses and too inexpensive for the classes, to misquote Irving Berlin.

What's more, there isn't enough pink spinel to change the situation dramatically. And besides scarcity, price and obscurity take their toll. Nevertheless, pink spinel deserves, and can support, more interest than it's getting.

THE BURMA MYSTIQUE

Like ruby and peridot, pink spinel at its best is a gem that is associated with Burma—and thus shares the benefit of origin in that fabled gem cornucopia. (So prized were its rubies that England invaded and annexed ruby-rich central Burma in 1888.) What can be called a mystique of place confers on many Burmese gems a special aura that allows them to command a premium just for being from Burma. No doubt, Burma origin played some part in catapulting red spinel to such prominence among investors and collectors in recent years.

But that mystique has yet to rub off on pink spinel. To the contrary, some dealers think that playing up Burma origin with a gem as unpopular and as unknown as pink spinel is conning the public.

Is it? To connoisseurs, Burma locality is synonymous with the best that gems of certain species such as ruby, jadeite and cultured pearl can be. Since the same holds for pink spinel, there is certainly some justification to bring this premier gem locality into its sales, also.

Just sit with spinel dealers and listen to them talk about this gem. They usually assume that most spinels with deep to day-glow pinks come from Burma. Sri Lanka, by far the biggest source of pink spinel, is said to produce pastel colors, meaning that they have more subdued color and lighter tone. (As compensation, Sri Lankan stones tend to be less included.) Given Burma's unexcelled reputation, it is hardly surprising

PINK SPINEL

that some dealers boast that they don't ever carry Sri Lankan spinels. Gemologists contest such claims.

"What dealers probably mean when they say they don't stock Ceylonese pink spinel is that they don't stock namby-pamby pale stones," says eminent gemologist Robert Crowningshield of the Gemological Institute of America. "The trade may be simply calling fine colors Burmese. But to us in the lab, fine color in spinel doesn't mean any particular place. Origin is not the issue with spinel that it is with ruby or sapphire."

The Los Angeles dealer who owns the 3.5-carat stone shown in our photo says pretty much the same thing when asked to describe its origin. "Let's just say it's Burma color," he insists.

But whether referring to color or place, the association with Burma still carries a special connotation that puts pink spinel on a par with equally rare, but currently more coveted pink topaz. "Because of interest in red spinel, pink spinel has found enough of a footing in recent years to go beyond being a collector's stone," a Seattle dealer says. "It has earned a place in jewelry stores."

TANZANITE

At its breathtaking best, tanzanite looks the spitting image of Kashmir sapphire—exhibiting the rich, royal velvety blue those stones are prized for.

But costing a fraction of the price.

Only the merest hint of violet tips off experts that the stone is something else.

That "something else" is a blue zoisite, rechristened tanzanite by Tiffany's in 1969 to honor its one source, Tanzania, and considered by many the pride of this gem-rich East African country. "It's so good to know there is a stone that is still actively mined that gives you the 'Kashmir-blue' color which is the ultimate for blue in gemstones," says a New York cutter.

But the fact that some tanzanites resemble Kashmir sapphires doesn't fully explain the red-hot demand for 1- to 6-carat sizes in all shades of this presently plentiful zoisite. Indeed, the stone seems well on its way to becoming a jewelry store staple. "Any retailer who's into colored stones seems to want at least one ring with tanzanite in stock," says one dealer in Beverly Hills.

Obviously, price has a lot to do with tanzanite's success. It's far less expensive than the sapphire for which it often serves as a substitute—although very fine stones can command $1,000 per carat in retail stores.

In recent years, the best bargains in tanzanite have been found in currently unpopular sizes above 10 carats. The reason: the gem's status change from narrow-niche collector to broad-market consumer stone. Throughout the 1970s, collectors were the primary following for tanzanite. Since they bought stones as showpieces, they concentrated on very large sizes. But ever since investment gems crashed in 1981, collectors have been absent from the market, leaving retailers to take up the slack. The shift in tanzanite's audience has been accompanied by important shifts in demand and taste for this gem.

NOT A SAPPHIRE SUBSTITUTE

As retailers and jewelry manufacturers became the primary users of tanzanite, size preferences dropped decidedly below 10 carats into the 1- to 6-carat range. At the same time, the gem began to be appreciated far more for itself and far less as a sapphire substitute, once its principal market function.

This isn't to say that the old connoisseur color ideal for this gem, a Kashmir blue, was abandoned. But now there is greater admiration for tanzanites that don't ape fine sapphires, a factor slowly freeing the gem

TANZANITE

from its second-class status as a sapphire substitute. As a Los Angeles gem importer puts it, "There is a need for a violet-blue stone in between, say, sapphire and amethyst that tanzanite fills." On those grounds, she continues, "We feel that violetish tanzanites are as beautiful and deserve as much praise as the 'Kashmir-blue' ones."

Not everyone agrees with this judgment, and there is a radical split in taste between marketers of tanzanite. Some middle-of-the-roaders say the division boils down to economics rather than aesthetics. "It is going too far to say that Kashmir-blue and strong violetish-blue tanzanites are equals," says one of them. "The Kashmir color is finer, but the violetish stones are attractive and need no apologies. More important, the economics of cutting will always dictate a preponderance of these stones."

WEIGHT VERSUS BEAUTY

He's right. Strong violetish blue will always dominate market supply, but it's not nature's doing. The truth is there could be far more Kashmir-blue tanzanites. Often, it's simply a matter of cutting the rough a certain way.

Tanzanite is a trichroic stone. This means that it gives off different colors when viewed from different directions, or axes. In tanzanite, one axis is blue, another violetish and the last reddish brown or bronze. When buying tanzanite rough, cutters look for strong trichroism, plus, of course, intense colors, as desirable signs. After cutting, the stone is heated (in a manner similar to aquamarine) to induce a permanent color change—usually from a brownish to a bluish color. The stones with the strongest reddish brown in them before heating bake to the deepest blue. Without heating, tanzanite would be unmarketable.

But coaxing the ultimate blue out of a stone is finally up to the cutter. And here's where economics enter the picture. Ordinarily, the best blue comes from cutting along the blue axis. But cutting along the blue axis usually means sacrificing the most rough. In order to get more yield, most cutters cut along other axes. This often produces steely-blue or strongly violetish stones which cannot be re-cut afterward to produce a bluer color.

Since the cutting is irrevocable, small compromises are big matters affecting Kashmir-blue stones. If the cutting is not absolutely correct, stones are unable to hold their color in a wide variety of lighting conditions. That's why some cutters insist on seeing the stones in incandescent light before making an offer for them. Should the stone turn

TANZANITE

violet, their offering price is much lower than if it retains its strong blue color.

Nevertheless, a growing number of cutters resent residual snobbery against the strongly violetish stones that result when they cut for weight, especially now that such stones are more acceptable. As they see it, by cutting for weight, they keep down the final cost of tanzanite to jewelers and consumers.

Maybe so, purists point out, but for a little more money consumers could have stones with a blue that is among the most cherished gem hues in the world. "The Kashmir-blue color is an ideal that can more readily be realized with tanzanite today than sapphire," one hard-liner says. "It's a shame to see so many stones deprived of the chance to embody that ideal."

Stones that do embody the Kashmir ideal have been known to fool jewelers—sometimes with dire consequences. Jewelry benchmen with no gemological training who have mistaken tanzanite for sapphire have frequently destroyed stones. The reason: Tanzanite, which is softer and more fragile than sapphire, cracks, and on occasion shatters, when exposed to extreme temperatures or sudden temperature changes. So any time you take a piece of tanzanite jewelry in for a repair, make sure the benchman is told that he's working with tanzanite. What's more, given tanzanite's delicate nature, it is probably better off set in, say, a pendant than a ring. Everyday wear on the hand practically guarantees scuffing up these stones over time—something that requires periodic repolishing by a cutter to fix.

BLUE TOPAZ

Dealers don't like to admit it but blue topaz has given aquamarine, its blue beryl double, a hard time in the last few years.

Indeed, aqua that once fetched hundreds of dollars per carat in jewelry stores has dropped considerably in price because look-alike blue topaz was selling readily to the trade for a fraction of the cost. Jewelry makers who couldn't see any difference between the two stones but price took to topaz.

So did retailers, especially when they realized that for around one-twentieth the cost of medium-to-better aqua they could buy all they wanted of deep-shade blue topaz. That was just too good an opportunity to pass up. As a result, a lot of U.S. aqua sellers have had to add blue topaz to their inventories over the last few years. They were joined by hundreds of dealers all over the world racing to ride the huge blue topaz wave to America's shores.

And what a wave it has been. Incredible as it may seem, blue topaz has become the biggest selling non-traditional colored stone in this country. But while the gem has also scored big abroad, passion for it in foreign markets hasn't crippled aqua sales as it has done here. Dealers believe that consumers in sophisticated gem-consuming countries like Japan clearly see blue topaz as a novelty and not an aqua substitute. In America, however, it is regarded as a colored stone staple. And since topaz is America's November birthstone, many jewelers now feature the blue variety instead of the more expensive golden variety.

MIXED EMOTIONS

Despite the success of blue topaz, many dealers who sell it do so with ambivalence, stocking the gem, without much enthusiasm, to accommodate customers. Granted, these dealers admit, the stone gives the look of fine aquamarine at a fraction of that gem's price. But the fact that topaz color is produced at will using irradiation riles them. Somehow this makes the gem more a product of the laboratory than nature.

Trade ambivalence about topaz is evident in the marketing and merchandising of the gem. Few retailers even bother to tell the public that the blue topaz it is buying by the ton owes its color to either a nuclear reactor or a linear accelerator.

Some see such non-disclosure as a coverup of radioactivity health hazards. That's just not so. Interviews with treaters, dealers and government officials lead us to conclude that blue topaz poses no danger whatsoever. First of all, stones treated in ways that leave residual radioactivity are quarantined (usually anywhere from three months to one year)

BLUE TOPAZ

until levels read ultra-conservatively low. By the time these stones get to jewelry stores, radioactivity is unmeasurable with conventional geiger counters. What's more, even when the Nuclear Regulatory Commission (NRC), which licenses reactors in this country where topaz is treated, ran radioactivity tests of irradiated blue topaz using ultra-expensive and sensitive measuring devices, it found no cause for concern.

So why neglect to tell the public about irradiation? The answer, we think, lies in the fact that the gem is a high-tech hybrid that transcends all conventional classifications. On one hand, the stone is natural, starting life as super-abundant colorless or ever-so-slightly tinted topaz from places like Brazil and Sri Lanka. On the other hand, its color is entirely manmade, due to a combination of irradiation (which incites the color change) and heating (which stabilizes the change).

Now topaz isn't the first gem to be safely and permanently colored by irradiation. Diamonds have been subjected to this process since the late 1940s. What is new about irradiated topaz is its sheer profusion and its phenomenal success.

Given the ubiquity of blue topaz, there are some jewelers who refuse to stock it. They fear that there's over-saturation of the market and that it threatens this gem's future. "It's a fad," a carriage trade jeweler says, one that reminds him, as it does others, of the Linde synthetic star sapphire craze of the 1950s.

BIRTH OF THE BLUES

Blue topaz specialists resent the comparison of their product to the Linde star. That makes it seem as if blue topaz is entirely a product of the laboratory. Defenders of blue topaz like to remind critics of the stone that aquamarine, blue topaz's near-twin, also depends upon lab-enhancement for its color. Neither stone, they argue, is true-blue.

That's a bit of an overstatement. Although aqua is commonly heated to remove green, exposure to low-level heat is far from the same thing as exposure to electron and neutron bombardment. This vast difference between aqua and blue topaz in degree of reliance on technological enhancement leaves the latter gem in an ambiguous position—neither fish nor fowl.

Perhaps it begs for a new gemological classification: that of processed gemstone. In any case, dealer annoyance with the gem seems somewhat groundless. Those who complain that blue topaz has a suspicious mass-produced color-sameness possible only with irradiation are probably not aware that only 20% to 30% of the stones irradiated turn a desirable

BLUE TOPAZ

color. True, the eyeshadow names like "sky blue" given to various irradiated topaz hues suggests paint-chip color consistency. But such, topaz specialists assure us, is not the case. Instead, these terms are market shorthand for various irradiation techniques used.

Treaters who want deep aqua-blue colors use neutron bombardment in a nuclear reactor and market the final product under the name "London blue." Neutron treatment is the only means by which to produce smaller calibrated stones with deep color. If this technique is used, stones fall under NRC jurisdiction. Current NRC rules require that neutron bombardment done in this country, regardless of gem species, be performed only by NRC-licensed reactors. If stones are reactor-treated abroad, their U.S. importers must be licensed by the NRC to bring them into the country.

However, blue topaz irradiated in any manner other than neutron bombardment escapes NRC scrutiny. That's because other techniques involve non-residual radioactivity for which measuring decay (or half lives) is not important. After neutron bombardment, the most common irradiation technique used to color topaz is electron bombardment in a linear accelerator. In general, this technique produces the lighter shades of sky blue.

More recently, topaz producers have combined reactor and accelerator treatment to produce an attractive color we find reminiscent of blue zircon, a stone that owes its color to heating. Ironically, several importers told us the color of these stones was "fake."

Treaters think this reaction is more psychological than aesthetic. They note that tanzanite, a brownish-purplish zoisite heated to turn a desirable blue, is almost never found naturally in its blue state. So what's the difference between brownish zoisite and colorless topaz? Except for price, it's looking more and more like there isn't an answer to that question.

PINK TOPAZ

Ever since blue topaz, the copious and affordable gem that owes its deep-menthol color to irradiation, took the jewelry world by storm in the mid-1980s, the trade has been hoping that zapping could make pink topaz just as plentiful and inexpensive.

But it is one thing to coax deep-blue from dirt-cheap, somewhat abundant colorless topaz and another to coax deep-pink from not-so-cheap, not-so-common precious topaz. Although rumors abound that treaters are using irradiation to produce pink topaz, we have yet to confirm a single one of them.

Besides, dealers versed in home and office color-craft have long been heating precious topaz, especially flesh and salmon-colored stones, to remove obtrusive browns and oranges and render stones permanently pink. This method is generations old. What's more, it's pretty low-tech, requiring heat sources like a gas flame that are no more sophisticated than a wino's Sterno can (although we caution readers against any experimentation with heat treatment to change the color of their stones).

Because heating is relatively easy to perform once one is trained to do it, it can be assumed that any pink topaz from Brazil, this gem's main modern producer, is colored more by man than nature. (This assumption does not seem to hold for pink topaz from the Ural Mountains of Russia, the leading source for this gem a century ago and the origin country of the term "imperial topaz"—so named to honor the Czar. Incidentally, the species-name topaz may derive from the Sanskrit word for fire, *tapas*, a reference to its fiery orange color.)

So if both pink and blue topaz are color enhanced, why is the former so very much more expensive than the latter?

The answer is simple: Topaz transformable into pink stones costs a lot more than topaz transformable into blue ones. The reason it costs more is limited supply. Not necessarily of precious topaz, but precious topaz with an essential coloring agent: chromium, the same trace element responsible for red in ruby. Relatively few stones from Brazil have this trace element in enough quantity for what dealers there call "pinking." On the other hand, gem-rich Pakistan holds great promise as a source of pink topaz—much of it so purely pink to begin with no enhancement is needed.

BRAZILIAN BLUSH

Although the colorless topaz that can be turned aqua-blue is found throughout the world, the topaz that can be turned pink seems only to come from Brazil, much of it from one mining locality: Oro Preto.

PINK TOPAZ

According to one treatment whiz, stones most responsive to heat are the intense fiery-golden kind known as imperial topaz. "I've never seen a piece of imperial topaz that didn't turn pink," he says. Unfortunately, this material is so expensive that it doesn't pay to heat it. So dealers experiment with less costly material.

At present, such experimentation is pretty much hit or miss. John Koivula, chief gemologist at the Gemological Institute of America, Santa Monica, Calif., says dealers look for affordable crystals, usually ones that show a pink color surrounded by brown and orange when viewed down the C-axis (length). That's a pretty good indicator of convertability to pink. What these dealers are seeing, Koivula explains, are "concentration zones of chromium coloration." Heat burns off the brown that masks these zones and leaves stones anywhere from sweet lilac to deep, reddish violet.

When lilac, far more often the result than reddish violet, stones resemble the fine bright kunzites seen recently from Afghanistan but cost far more. If you don't mind the mild presence of orange and brown which gives stones a salmon color, you'll find pink topaz far more affordable.

Of course, there is always the chance that extensive experimentation heating precious topaz may yet reveal a way to convert far more stones to pink. But the risks are high. Heating can fracture commonly encountered carbon dioxide inclusions. Further, many stones may not have enough chromium to ever go beyond the pale.

Consequently, selection of heating candidates must become more scientific. Koivula believes this may happen as dealers discover and subject candidate crystals to chromium content analysis before "pinking." This involves use of sophisticated technology such as neutron activation or microprobes that measure amounts of trace elements.

PINKS FROM PAKISTAN
If topaz finds in Pakistan prove significant, heating of precious topaz to create much-needed pink stones may become unnecessary. According to Cap Beesley, president of American Gemological Laboratories in New York and a United Nations consultant to Pakistan's gem exploration venture, the country is producing "all-natural purplish-red stones that are unique in color and intensity." Priced by the government at levels far above those of the finest Brazilian stones, these magnificent gems appeal only to a handful of collectors.

Although far less expensive, Pakistan's more abundant brownish pastel-pink and apricot-orange topazes are still priced way above current

PINK TOPAZ

market levels for comparable Brazilian stones. "The prices reflect the tremendous start-up costs of full-scale gem exploration and mining in Pakistan," Beesley explains. "Nonetheless, they are a bit off the wall."

Officials of Pakistan's government-run gem sales division try to justify higher prices for their stones by saying they are untreated. But this may not be a matter of choice. Beesley believes the Pakistanis might be trying to make a virtue of a defect. "From what I understand, their orangy-brown stones don't turn pink when subjected to heat, perhaps due to the presence of vanadium along with chromium," he says. "So suddenly all the topaz is being proclaimed free of treatment."

Whatever the case, lack of enhancement is not liable to mean much to the trade or public, accustomed as both have become to heating and irradiation, especially of topaz. Nevertheless, the best of Pakistan's pinks are in a class by themselves and merit some sort of premium on that basis—unless geologists there hit upon some fairly significant pockets soon.

Beesley feels confident they will. "The pink stones seen so far come from a hillock in the middle of a flat alluvial plain," he explains. "The next stage of exploration will take teams of mining engineers into the mountains that surround this area. If the vein continues, Pakistan could some day become equal in importance to Brazil for pink topaz."

PRECIOUS TOPAZ

If you had visited the Rio de Janeiro offices of a gem dealer acquaintance of mine in mid-1982, chances are you would have seen several pieces of precious topaz taped to the sun-drenched windows.

"You didn't dare buy polished topaz then without subjecting it to fade-testing," he says. "That was when the topaz irradiation scare was at its height. And the best way to test for irradiation was to let stones sit for a couple of hours in the very intense Brazilian sun."

Today his office windows are once again bare, largely because the irradiated topaz scare has subsided. But, if nothing else, the precious topaz scare of 1982-83 provides an important cautionary tale about the dangers of indiscriminate, undisclosed gemstone treatment.

During the scare, topaz prices dropped at least 50% below record highs reached in 1981 when topaz, much of it second-rate, briefly became the leading Brazilian investment gem. That year, also, many dealers discovered irradiation as a means to pump up supplies of the gem's much-prized deep orange and reddish-orange colors.

Unfortunately, the fine colors produced by irradiation (as opposed to heating, a gem enhancement technique used for topaz whose results are permanent) tended to fade, a fact which many Brazilians who sold this treated material failed to disclose. To make things worse, importers here feared these gems might pose a health hazard. Meanwhile, investor demand for topaz petered out.

The three-way collision between investor drop-out, importer paranoia and market glut in late 1981 "left Brazilian dealers burnt far worse than their stones," says a Miami gem importer. "Topaz suddenly became the most stigmatized Brazilian gem. No one trusted the stone or the Brazilians who sold it. This distrust sent prices crashing."

Today importer distrust of topaz is largely a thing of the past. Once-shaky prices have regained upward momentum, especially for pink and pinkish stones which have shared heartily in the current fashion vogue for pink gems.

A SYNONYM FOR YELLOW

Topaz is perhaps the most misused name in the gem world, often confused with a good many other yellow/golden/brown species, from golden sapphire to citrine. The confusion is deepest with citrine, a far more common and less expensive golden quartz whose finest color is a reddish-brown madeira very reminiscent of some fine topaz. Very often, too, pale brownish-yellow stones called smoky quartz are sold as "smoky topaz." Unfortunately, these confusions are perpetuated by many jewelers—

PRECIOUS TOPAZ

sometimes on the advice of suppliers and sales reps who themselves don't know any better. A simple lesson in Portuguese, the language of Brazil, should be enough to end the confusion once and for all.

In Brazil, miners and dealers use the catch-all term *topazio*, meaning yellow, to describe almost any gem that is basically or strongly yellow. In most cases where the term *topazio* is used by itself, it is understood the gem being referred to is citrine or, perhaps, a quartz family relative. Often dealers will specify a mining locality such as Rio Grande or Bahia to make it clear from which area the citrine comes. To distinguish more highly prized precious topaz from quartz, dealers use the phrase *topazio imperiale*. That's why precious topaz is so often called "imperial topaz" in this country. It is quite simply a literal translation of the Portuguese phrase used to separate topaz from quartz.

Since the introduction of the phrase "imperial topaz" into this country, however, the term has become more precise, less broad, implying, as the word "imperial" can't help but do, finer grades and greater cost. But just what are the finer grades of a gem that runs a wide color range from yellow and brown through orange, pink and red—even, occasionally, lavender and violet—to blue? Some history may help to clarify the meaning of the term "imperial," as opposed to "precious" topaz.

The original derivation of the term "imperial" stems from the discovery of pink topaz in Russia during the 19th century. The gem was instantly so coveted that ownership was restricted to the Czar, his family and those to whom he gave it as a gift. Hence the term "imperial." For many years after it was coined, the term became generic for all topaz. But gradually dealers confined its meaning to a certain range of rich colors and saturate color intensities.

Today it is conceded that the term "imperial" refers, among connoisseurs, to stones with sherry-red, deep pink and reddish-orange colors and generally excludes less intense but still beautiful peach-orange and medium golden hues. These latter colors are considered "precious." As stones become progressively yellower and browner, they become mere topaz.

THE CURRENT MARKET

At present, manufacturers are using smaller well-cut, eye-clean topaz, generally between 3 and 6 carats. To keep jewelry pieces affordable, jewelry makers usually avoid true imperial topaz with its fiery reddish-orange color in favor of golden to peachy colors, often with considerable pink overtones. Jewelry manufacturer demand tapers off sharply over

PRECIOUS TOPAZ

10 carats, although the action has picked up somewhat from what it was. On the whole, the worst is over for topaz. Prices for better-to-fine grades have rebounded 40% to 50% since the topaz market touched bottom in 1983.

One contributing factor to the topaz turnaround has been the enormous popularity of pink as a fashion color in the past few years and the insatiable demand for pink gems in jewelry as a consequence. The rush for pink has sent prices for very fine to top-grade orange-red to sherry-red topaz soaring. Fortunately, more moderate priced topaz has also benefited from the pink gem craze because pastel shades are just as desirable today as intense ones.

This turn of events could be a big break for topaz. While topaz does not take to irradiation as far as producing permanent pink and orange colors, many orange stones with a strong pink color component can be made all-pink using very low levels of heat. Although this color enhancement technique has been used for decades, it has become the focus of heightened interest as dealers experiment with it on inexpensive slightly pinkish-orange to salmon-color stones, hoping to generate a greater abundance of pink topaz.

So far, this technique has not proved a miracle worker. Dealers who have tried the method say that the outcome of heating depends on two factors: the overall color intensity of the original stone and the amount of pink in it. If not sufficiently saturate in color to begin with, heat will, at best, remove the orange, leaving a light all-pink end color. To make rich-color pink stones, you need rich-color pinkish-orange stones. Alas, the deep-color stones needed to make such pinks are too costly, forcing dealers to take their chances with stones that are far cheaper and lighter.

CALIFORNIA TOURMALINE

Just as East Africa is the brave new world of gem mining today, America was her counterpart a century ago.

Certainly, the discovery of tourmaline in Southern California in 1898 touched off as much excitement in the international jewelry market as did the discovery of tanzanite and tsavorite in Kenya and Tanzania in the 1960s.

Tiffany's, which played a major role in elevating the two East African unknowns to front-rank gems, played an equally important role in the success of California tourmaline. Tiffany's then, as later, was among the world's most adventuresome jewelry stores, ever alert to new gem discoveries for which it could negotiate exclusive or near-exclusive distribution rights.

How it did so with California tourmaline would make a riveting movie, one filled with as much action and intrigue as any about the state's far more famous gold rush.

So let's return briefly to those days of yesteryear when gemologists (those at Tiffany's', anyway) were expected to act like Indiana Joneses in the line of duty.

A SAN DIEGO SAGA

It is a tribute to the beauty of California tourmaline that around 1902 Tiffany went through so much to get it. At that time, and for a long time after, California was to tourmaline what South Africa was to diamonds.

Between 1898 and 1914 especially, California's San Diego County was unrivaled for production of this gem (although stones were reported from, among other places, Brazil, Burma and Ceylon). Indeed, close to 100 tons of gem and ornamental tourmaline came from one mine, known as the Himalaya in Mesa Grande, an amount estimated to comprise at least 80% of the area's entire output in the prewar period.

Tiffany's virtually cornered the market on California's tourmaline. And it did so in a manner more reminiscent of a buccaneer than a gentleman. One of its employees, gemologist J.L. Tannenbaum, jumped the previous mine owner's claim. Or so a 1904 court judgment against Tannenbaum suggests.

From the first time he laid eyes on the new California tourmalines in 1898, Tannenbaum seems to have been a man possessed. By 1902, when he could not find the exact whereabouts of the new deposit, he decided to go to San Diego himself. As Indiana Jones might have done, Tannenbaum concealed the objective of his travels, pretending instead to be a consumptive looking to buy a mountain cabin for his health.

CALIFORNIA TOURMALINE

And, he might have added, for his wealth. Not surprisingly, he found an ideal rest site near the Himalaya tourmaline mine.

In no time at all, the "tubercular" began to work the Himalaya mine, provoking a lawsuit from its owner, Gail Lewis (who Tannenbaum maintained had improperly filed his mine claim). Eventually, Tannenbaum had to pay Lewis $40,000 to make him relinquish title to the mine.

If Lewis could have foreseen the tourmaline yields that lay ahead, it is doubtful he would have ever sold his mine. According to various accounts, the 1902-1910 production from the entire Mesa Grande district was worth between $750,000 and $800,000. Since more than 80% of this material came from the Himalaya mine, it is safe to say Tannenbaum and his backers (presumably Tiffany's) profited handsomely from the takeover.

THE SINO/SAN DIEGO CONNECTION

California tourmaline had friends in high and faraway places. The most important of them, by far, was Empress Tzu Hsi of China. Her love of carved tourmalines made China practically the sole underpinning of the turn-of-the-century tourmaline market. When news of California's prodigious tourmaline production made its way to her court, she immediately sent emissaries to various mining districts. The resulting Sino/San Diego tourmaline pacts contributed heavily to prosperity there, so much so that when the Chinese government collapsed in 1912, the tourmaline market capsized with it.

Ironically, the importance of San Diego tourmaline mining today is once again tied, at least in part, to a strongly revived market for tourmaline carvings. Cutters like Gerhard Becker of West Germany's famed gem-cutting city, Idar-Oberstein, have earned world renown for their beautiful bird and animal tourmaline figurines, many of which use California material.

For sure, tourmaline mining in California is nothing like it was around 1910 when rapid mining had already exhausted most of the area's surface riches and forced development of far more expensive underground workings. After World War II, the far cheaper cost of production in Brazil catapulted that country to its current No. 1 status as tourmaline producer.

But California has longevity and lore going for it. After all, says a California gem dealer who first made his reputation as a tourmaline miner, "There aren't many gems for which America can claim such historical leadership in terms of mining."

CALIFORNIA TOURMALINE

IN THE PINK

Besides providing carving material, San Diego County is still an important locality for facetable tourmaline. As our photo shows, the color variety is wide. But, basically, California tourmaline comes in shades of pink which vary from mine to mine. The famed Himalaya mine, on which the dealer has held leases since 1978, was extraordinarily bountiful until May 1985. Since then, production has been spotty. Nevertheless, the mine has given one California gem company a two-year backlog of fine pinks and bi-colored stones—suitable for both cutting and carving.

At its best, the color of better Himalayan stones is a hot bubblegum pink. Usually, however, the color is a softer pastel pink. Occasionally, some California pinks will boast a purplishness that makes them easily mistakable for superb rhodolites. But no matter which shade of pink you buy, these stones are almost invariably included, even the blue ribbon ones.

Unique to the Himalaya mine, says one dealer, are eye-clean, green/pink tourmalines that are almost always cut in elongated rectangles (due to the composition of the original rough).

Last, and unfortunately least, there are a few beautiful, hard-to-describe green tourmalines from California. But don't get your hopes up about ordering them. Supplies are exceedingly thin and will be thinner yet if the public learns how inexpensive they are.

CHROME TOURMALINE

Are the wives of the late African miner Ali Giowatta once again on speaking terms?

One way to tell, say observers of the Tanzanian social scene, is to watch the supply of chrome tourmaline.

Giowatta, permitted by his religion to be a polygamist, owned the world's only two chrome tourmaline mines, both located in northern Tanzania. When he died in December 1980, a bitter battle for control of the mines broke out between his three wives. This feud brought the mines' already sporadic production to a halt. The world had to depend on dealer backlogs of this gem, many of them in Idar-Oberstein, Germany's centuries-old cutting center.

When "chromes" (as they are sometimes called) began popping up in greater numbers in Nairobi, Kenya—East Africa's chief gem trading city—back in 1984, it was assumed that domestic tranquility had been restored among Giowatta's heirs. True, some argued that the pickup in supply had more to do with the fact that Tanzania, a socialist country, had opened its borders to its capitalist neighbor, Kenya. But since the bettering of border ties took place in 1983 without a resumption of chrome tourmaline plenty until a year afterward, closer harmony between Giowatta's wives won credit for the improved flow of chrome tourmaline.

The harmony does not seem to have lasted long. Six months later, chromes were as scarce as before. Ever since, production of the gem has been sporadic as ever, just enough to keep aficionados loyal and prices the highest paid for any tourmaline variety.

Those prices may seem baffling until one examines a fine chrome tourmaline. Top specimens of this gem exhibit a green that tempts confusion with fine tsavorite and rivals emerald. Even so, some dealers wonder how chrome tourmaline became the most expensive tourmaline in the world. The main reason is the gem's East African origin and that region's reputation for somewhat pricey green gems.

A CLEAN GREEN

Like East Africa's most widely respected gem, tsavorite garnet, chrome tourmaline is noted for a rich, bright, clean green that specialists insist is visually distinctive and has no real counterpart among other tourmalines. Indeed, novices are apt to mistake fine chrome tourmaline for fine tsavorite.

They shouldn't feel bad, however. So do the experts. "The finest quality chrome tourmalines are only distinguishable from tsavorite with the aid

CHROME TOURMALINE

of a gemological instrument such as a refractometer," says a Bermuda-based African gem expert. (The refractive index of chrome tourmaline is usually 1.62-1.64 while that of tsavorite is 1.74.)

Very recently, some superb stones have tempted comparison to very fine Colombian emerald. The Bermuda dealer, who spends much of his time in Nairobi, reports that some newer material sports a "lovely bluish-green cast." One such stone, on display at the recent American Gem Trade Association show in New York, resembled a spectacular emerald. Weighing more than 8 carats, it fetched close to $1,000 per carat for its owner, a New York dealer—the highest price we have heard of for a chrome tourmaline.

But it was an outstandingly beautiful stone, perhaps one of a kind (we have yet to see its second).

More commonly, very fine chrome tourmalines lean more toward the yellow than the blue end of the spectrum. But whether yellowish or bluish, their chromium content is what gives them their bright, sharp, vivid color. Jewelers can test for chromium content with a Chelsea filter. Under the filter, chrome-laden stones will show flashes of red or orangy red.

The Chelsea test is the main way dealers confirm the East African origin of tourmaline. Far more abundant green tourmalines from Brazil, Afghanistan, Maine and California are colored primarily by iron. So when these stones are subjected to a Chelsea filter test, their color remains green.

Even without a filter, dealers versed in tourmaline say "chromes" have a unique visual appeal. At their best, they boast an almost corrosively brilliant color. Of course, this uniqueness is reflected in their prices which generally, says one California retailer, are three times that of any other green tourmaline.

CAUGHT IN THE MIDDLE

Although chrome tourmaline is scarcer than tsavorite, it is not plagued by the size problem of that garnet. Chrome tourmaline occurs fairly frequently in sizes up to 10 carats while tsavorite is extremely hard to find in sizes over 2 carats. For this reason, top-grade tsavorites around 2 carats easily command 10 times what kindred-caliber chrome tourmalines around 2 carats will cost.

Yet demand for chrome tourmaline is probably less than one-hundredth that for tsavorite. Why? "Jewelers don't think of chrome tourmaline as a bargain compared to tsavorite," says a New Jersey importer.

CHROME TOURMALINE

"They think of it as very expensive tourmaline."

This is not to say that chrome tourmaline doesn't have its followers. Usage is increasing among jewelers and jewelry manufacturers. Virtually unknown before 1970, this tourmaline has now become the color standard for deep green in this gem. As said before, it has something to do with East Africa and the special aura that surrounds its gems, especially the green ones.

A word of caution is necessary here, though. Many chrome tourmalines do not possess the fine green we are describing and for which we are quoting prices. According to the Bermuda dealer, only one of the two Tanzanian mines that produce this gem can be counted on for a fairly steady but thin flow of fine stones. It is called the Landanai mine and its stones are usually free of the brownish overtones that mar the tourmalines from its more productive sister mine.

Brownishness isn't the only problem with chrome tourmaline. Often stones will be so saturate with green that they appear blackish or over dark. Unless price is your prime consideration, we advise steering clear of either brownish or blackish stones. "If you must compromise," a dealer says, "go with lighter, livelier stones. The dark, somber-colored ones are almost impossible to sell."

One last tip: Expect stones to be eye-clean. "A small wispy veil might be okay," a dealer advises, "but stones shouldn't be what you would call included."

TSAVORITE

Despite Tiffany connections and a large connoisseur following, tsavorite is becoming something of a has-been. And the very thing that should be helping the faltering career of this green garnet, strong family ties to much-coveted demantoid garnet, is hurting it. Indeed, tsavorite seems cursed by déjà vu as it follows in the footsteps of that other green garnet.

Although demantoid took the jewelry salons of Paris and New York by storm after its discovery in Russia's Ural Mountains in 1868, the vogue didn't survive the Victorian era because mining lasted less than 30 years. Many dealers predict a repeat of green garnet history as mining of tsavorite, an equally captivating look-alike grossular garnet found in Kenya a century later, threatens to die out even more quickly.

"Tsavorite is the 20th century's demantoid," declares one dealer versed in African gems. "Of between 40 and 50 mines worked since the late 1960s, only one of any importance is now operating. The other few are small and their production of fine stones is practically nil."

But Campbell Bridges, the mining geologist who is credited with having discovered tsavorite and persuading Tiffany's (the first and foremost booster of demantoid) to promote it, dismisses such judgments as premature. "There's enough tsavorite coming from Kenya to make it a genuinely commercial gemstone," he says.

That's debatable. By Bridges' own count, only four tsavorite mining ventures have output of any consequence, hardly enough, at this point, to guarantee a flow of the garnet anything like that of 15 years ago. And even then, tsavorite wasn't all that abundant. As production has dwindled steadily throughout the 1980s, dealer pessimism has increased inversely.

Nevertheless, specialists in East African stones cling to the diehard belief that the supply of tsavorite will some day soon return to old levels. After all, they maintain, politics, not geology, is what has held back tsavorite.

More likely, both factors are to blame.

A VISIT TO THE BUSH
Imagine yourself in a flat, arid grassland, studded with hills and extinct volcanoes, that stretches roughly 40 miles from the Taita hills of Kenya into next-door Tanzania. Every once in a while you may see a farm, but for the most part, this is snake-infested bush where prowling lions are not an unusual sight. This area, approximately 800 square miles in size, is tsavorite country.

Tsavorite (a name Tiffany marketers derived from Kenya's famous

TSAVORITE

Tsavo Park in 1974) is found only in East Africa. Because of the region's geology, described by a Bermuda dealer as "warped and convoluted," tsavorite is a maverick mineral. Deposits, perhaps "pockets" would be a better word, are usually small and very unpredictable. "Seams just pinch out without leaving any indication of where they pick up again," the Bermuda dealer explains. "It's very frustrating, to say the least."

As befits such tortuous, tortured deposits, rough crystals show evidence of massive abuse while in the ground. Due to tremendous volcanic heat and pressure, it is rare that dealers find sections of rough more than ¼ inch in length that are clean enough to cut. The remaining areas of the crystal are usually shattered and battered. Indeed, dealers work with what are best described as crystal pieces and slivers. Natives even call these irregularly shaped roughs "potatoes."

Given such brutalized rough, it is hardly surprising that cut tsavorites over 3 carats are exceedingly rare.

To get at this tsavorite, especially that embedded in the hills that dot the region, takes expensive earth-removal equipment run on ultra-expensive diesel fuel. All this requires lots of venture capital, a commodity that doesn't flow as readily into Africa nowadays as it did in the 1970s.

Should mining money start flowing again, dealers are sure that tsavorite production would reach old peaks. "It's not like there's no more tsavorite in the ground," says one stone importer. "If you'd ever been in the mining region, you'd have seen tsavorite outcroppings all over the place."

A GREEN OF ITS OWN

Nevertheless, doubts about the future of tsavorite have already begun to take their toll. Not exactly a mainstream gem, tsavorite has found wide acceptance mostly among custom jewelers. But even some of these tsavorite loyalists have had to turn to alternative stones like chrome tourmaline, another East African gem.

"It's a real 'Catch-22' situation," worries a California dealer. "The inadequacy of production leads to decreased demand. Decreased demand then discourages further production."

Tsavorite must break out of its present downward supply-demand spiral if it is to keep the small but solid jewelry niche it has earned for itself. Accordingly, miners are trying to boost demand. One of them is making the rounds of American gem dealers and jewelry manufacturers pitching clean, well-cut, good-color tsavorite in small sizes as an ideal alternative to emerald. "It's cheaper, harder and more brilliant than emerald, plus it's untreated [many emeralds are oiled to mask tiny cracks which may break their surface]," he stresses. "That makes it a far better gem to pair up with diamonds."

Interested buyers invariably respond to the miner with questions about supply. Geologist Bridges estimates that present Kenyan tsavorite ventures can provide 2,500 carats a month of decent material in sizes up to 33 points on a steady basis for the foreseeable future. "I know the caratage is a drop in the bucket compared to emerald," he concedes, "but it's a basis for the beginning of a manufacturer commitment."

No matter what happens with jewelry manufacturers, however, tsavorite is likely to stay a favorite of gem collectors. For one thing, it boasts almost non-stop price appreciation since the early 1970s. One reason for collector interest, a reason Bridges is trying to exploit with jewelry makers, is that tsavorite compares favorably to emerald. "It's the gem emerald should have been, equal in color and superior in every other regard," he says.

When buying tsavorite, consumers have every right to expect eye-clean stones. With regard to color, jewelers should look for a green very similar to that found in imperial jade. Failing that, stones with what one cutter calls "a lime Jell-O green" are acceptable. But avoid stones that are a light soda-bottle green or overly blackish and dark—even though they cost far less than deeper green garnets. The point is this: Tsavorite has a reputation for showing green at its best. So although it is nowhere near as expensive as comparable-grade emerald, it costs enough for purchasers to insist that it possess fine color.

TURQUOISE

This sky-blue copper derivative, so important to the ancient Egyptians and Aztecs, has known better times.

Perhaps the best times of all for this gem were the late 1960s when social awareness briefly held more sway in U.S. fashion trends than did the social registry. Back then, Native American jewelry was powerfully in vogue and turquoise, the gem most associated with it, was hot.

But once so-called Native American jewelry started coming from Hong Kong and Taiwan, with its turquoise often plastic-treated or just plain plastic altogether, the gem's popularity nose dived. It didn't help matters when a major tribe of the Southwest was found to have mass-produced some of the silver and turquoise jewelry in Asia that it had been selling as handmade in the USA.

Such scandals devastated the reputation of a gem that is as strongly linked to centuries of skillful jewelry artisanry and other decorative arts as amber and ivory. Yet even with such scandals, there were still small but evidently gold-lined pockets of connoisseurship for this gem. A Los Angeles turquoise specialist recalls prices to Iranian collectors of as much as $2,000 per piece for top-echelon 15x20mm turquoise cabochons as late as 1976—three years before the fall of the Shah.

Now it is doubtful that the finest turquoise could fetch anywhere near that price—unless a part of an important piece of antique jewelry, say a fine Islamic ring dating from around 1200. The sad truth about this gem is that rampant adulteration, plus a profusion of fakes, has cost it much of the public's trust. But even without much-publicized high-tech shenanigans, turquoise would probably have difficulty commanding big bucks today.

PERSIA SPELLED A-R-I-Z-O-N-A
Like copper, the metal of which the gem is a byproduct, turquoise is abundant at a time when demand has slackened considerably. The end result: ravaged prices. Indeed, output from turquoise mines in Arizona alone, presently the gem's biggest producer, is said to be about 1,500 pounds a week. Most of this material is sent to Hong Kong and, increasingly, Italy for processing. But American dealers often get to skim off the best grades.

Although the U.S. Southwest is well-known for turquoise mining, Arizona is not the place most jewelers and connoisseurs think of when they think of turquoise. Very likely Iran—or, should we say Persia—comes to mind, for that country has for centuries been regarded as the premier source. And, in fact, the name turquoise, which means "Turkish," refers to the fact that prized Persian material was originally brought to Europe via Turkey.

Just for the record, however, the earliest known deposits of turquoise were found in Egypt, at least as far back as 2000 B.C. Ironically, grades were so poor that Egypt's gifted jewelry artisans were forced to develop a substitute composed of a quartz paste that was shaped to look like pieces of turquoise, then glazed a beautiful sky-blue color before being hardened in a fire oven. Called faience, these turquoise simulants fooled antiquities experts until very recently.

Given the largely mediocre quality of Egypt's Sinai-mined turquoise, it is hardly surprising that so few jewelers know of its role in history. Ancient Persia is widely believed to be the first, as well as the best, source of turquoise. And for many purists, it is the only source. That's why much of the fine turquoise sold today is sold as "Persian." Only it's not. Mining activity in Iran is negligible at best. "Most of the turquoise sold as Persian today really comes from America," the Los Angeles dealer says.

Now many readers might find this evidence of continued turquoise charlatanry. But, in reality, American turquoise boasts its own grand, but far less celebrated, heritage—a heritage Americans unconsciously honored when Indian jewelry was all the rage in the late '60s and early '70s.

MEMORIES OF MEXICO

Native American jewelry is primarily identified with three tribes: the Navajo, Pueblo and Zuni. Actually, however, turquoise veneration and use here reaches back centuries to the time when New Mexico, a major U.S. turquoise locality, was a part of the great Aztec empire of Mexico (1300 to 1520 A.D.).

To the Aztecs, turquoise was a commodity more valuable than gold and a principal decorative medium. Even after the fall of the Aztec empire to the Spaniards, turquoise maintained its importance to the Indians, despite brutal attempts by their oppressors to confiscate it.

Few know it, but to the Pueblo tribe turquoise is synonymous with political liberation. For more than a century, tribe members were forced to work both underground and open-pit turquoise mines for Mexico's Spanish conquerors. Then, in 1680, after a major mine cave-in killed scores of workers, the Indians refused to work. Instead, they staged a rebellion and drove the Spaniards from their lands.

Such victories over what today is called imperialism would have probably added even more to the pleasure of turquoise ownership back in

TURQUOISE

the Vietnam era. But the intricate involvement of turquoise in Mexican and U.S. political history was pretty much ignored then—and now. No wonder some turquoise zealots consider it a mark of alienation from our past that more reverence is given to the Persian than the American variety of this gem. But defenders of Persian turquoise say the preference is based, as it should be, on aesthetics.

THE BLUE-SKY IDEAL
Talk of ideal color in turquoise today is, admittedly, a little beside the point, since manufacturers here and abroad are reluctant to pay much for the oval, pear and round cabochons they buy. For the little they spend, they generally receive mild to medium sky-blue colors—rarely, if ever, the intense deep-blue azures extolled by the experts.

Given the extremely low prices of high-grade natural turquoise, it is surprising to find a thriving market in treated material. The market is as old as love of turquoise, starting with the faience imitations of ancient Egypt. But the ancient imitations made sense because the gem was then genuinely precious—not to mention scarce relative to demand.

By the late 19th century, however, when fine turquoise was quite inexpensive, the tricks played with turquoise were much harder to condone. The great American gemologist George Kunz caused a sensation when he exposed the infamous "Berlin-blue" dyeing technique about 1900. But detection didn't deter even more ingenious deceits.

That's the biggest threat to the turquoise market today: ever more clever forms of doctoring such as stabilization with polymer binders to increase durability. While polymerized turquoise is understandable given the fact that the gem is very soft and porous, some recent laboratory concoctions that contain as little as 5% of the actual mineral are not. Such fakes are especially hard to countenance given all the natural turquoise and natural-turquoise substitutes such as azurite and chrysocolla on hand at rock-bottom prices.